MOVIE
STARS

D1556357

EG37956

MOVIE STARS

An illustrated history of the stars of the silver screen, from
the best-loved musical and comedy stars to the dazzling screen
goddesses and action heroes, with over 200 photographs

DON SHIACH

southwater

EG34956

NWLC LEARNING CENTRE
EALING GREEN
791.43028092 SMI

This edition is published by Southwater

Southwater is an imprint of
Anness Publishing Ltd
Hermes House
88–89 Blackfriars Road, London SE1 8HA
tel. 020 7401 2077; fax 020 7633 9499
www.southwaterbooks.com; info@anness.com

© Anness Publishing Ltd 2005

UK agent: The Manning Partnership Ltd
tel. 01225 478444; fax 01225 478440
sales@manning-partnership.co.uk

UK distributor: Grantham Book Services Ltd
tel. 01476 541080; fax 01476 541061
orders@gbs.tbs-ltd.co.uk

North American agent/distributor:
National Book Network
tel. 301 459 3366; fax 301 429 5746
www.nbnbooks.com

Australian agent/distributor: Pan Macmillan Australia
tel. 1300 135 113; fax 1300 135 103
customer.service@macmillan.com.au

New Zealand agent/distributor: David Bateman Ltd
tel. (09) 415 7664; fax (09) 415 8892

All rights reserved. No part of this publication
may be reproduced, stored in a retrieval system,
or transmitted in any way or by any means,
electronic, mechanical, photocopying, recording
or otherwise, without the prior written permission
of the copyright holder.

A CIP catalogue record for this book
is available from the British Library.

Publisher: Joanna Lorenz
Editorial Director: Judith Simons
Project Editor: Felicity Forster
Designer: Peter Bailey–Proof Books
Production Controller: Claire Rae

Previously published as part of a larger volume, *The Movies*

10 9 8 7 6 5 4 3 2 1

CONTENTS

INTRODUCTION

When the movies began to emerge as a popular mass entertainment, there were no movie stars as we know them. Gradually, however, the hucksters who ran Hollywood saw the percentage in creating these luminaries of the silver screen to lure the paying public into the cinemas. They realized they could sell a picture on the strength of the star appearing in it: they would do a "Chaplin", "Pickford" or "Fairbanks" movie and then repeat the formula again and again. Soon Hollywood success depended partly on the pulling power of these personalities who were catapulted to world fame, despite the lack of talent many of them displayed.

ABOVE *Movie stars such as Bette Davis and Errol Flynn (seen here in* The Private Lives of Elizabeth and Essex) *had an aura created for them by the full-time publicity departments of the studio they worked for.*

Some observers of the mass media see something sinister in how stars are used in movies. Herbert Marcuse, the German-American philosopher, wrote the following about how star images were used in Hollywood: "They are no longer images of another way of life but rather freaks or types of the same life, serving as an affirmation rather than a negation of the established order." In other words, stars have an ideological function; they make life more palatable for us by ironing out

6

the contradictions and worries that inevitably work their way into even the sunniest of movies. For example, if a "good joe" star such as James Stewart is shown to be poor but happy with his lot and the American Way of Life, then it is more likely that we will be seduced into feeling the same way.

There is no doubt that stars convey meaning of one kind or another. They signify something "extra" in a movie, especially if they have created a star persona from numerous films. John Wayne signified a kind of macho integrity, promising straight-shooting and straight-talking. Henry Fonda carried an aura of incorruptibility with him into almost all of his movies; he was the personable, archetypal "liberal" star. Monroe encapsulated for many an innocent joy in sex, and for others a child-like vulnerability. All the major stars had their dominant persona, arousing the audience's expectations. Sometimes a star would be cast against "type", so occasionally Gregory Peck or even Fonda would play a villain, but even that is an

LEFT *Marilyn Monroe was photographed in every possible pose and from every angle in the attempt to create for her an aura of ultimate glamour.*

example of how star personas can be used, because casting "against type" is still dependent upon our expectations as an audience of what these stars signify and how we react to them.

During the heyday of the Hollywood studio system, there was an elaborate grooming process for potential stars. They generally had to be glamorous, above reproach, and recognizable American types. If the moguls considered that they were wanting in some area, then the remodelling process could be severe. Rita Hayworth, for example, had to have her hairline raised by an

ABOVE *This "candid" shot of stars David Niven and Ginger Rogers was released to the press by Universal-International to publicize a movie called* Magnificent Doll (1946). *Here the stars are meant to be earnestly discussing script matters.*

ABOVE *Photo opportunities were seized on avidly by the publicists. Here Janet Leigh and Carleton Carpenter pose for the camera with Forgan, a sedated lion.*

inch through electrolysis (a very painful exercise) because Harry Cohn, Columbia's boss, thought she would look better that way. Names were the first thing to go if an actor's real moniker did not fit: Marion Michael Morrison became John Wayne, Doris von Kappelhoff became Doris Day,

and Britain's Diana Fluck became Diana Dors. The fan magazines and gossip writers would be handed publicity material to boost the public's awareness of up-and-coming stars and, once they were established, their reputations would be protected and continually polished.

Under old Hollywood, the stars were constrained by seven-year contracts with options every six months to be picked up or dropped by the employing studio. This contract tied the stars to their employers; the option clauses were used to make them toe the line and force them to make the movies the studios wanted them to make. Bette Davis and Olivia de Havilland took on their studios in the courts in an attempt to break the feudal hold the moguls had over them. They helped break up the old studio system, and the stars were in time largely released from the tyranny of the long-term contract. Burt Lancaster and Kirk Douglas were two early examples of producer-stars who took a financial risk in their own films and formed companies to make independent productions, which they then sold to the studios to market and distribute.

Soon the major stars became enterprises in themselves – millions of dollars for a movie budget could be raised on one star name. Agents became enormously important because the really powerful ones could promise a package of several stars and probably a top director, a successful screenwriter and a commercial vehicle for them all to participate in. Contemporary stars such as George Clooney or Julia Roberts are as much businessmen and women as actors.

ABOVE *The importance of the black audience in the United States led to the creation of African-American stars such as Dorothy Dandridge and Harry Belafonte.*

ABOVE *Stars acquired off-screen reputations that were used by the producers to publicize their movies. The Rat Pack's aura – with Frank Sinatra, Dean Martin, Sammy Davis Jr and Peter Lawford as the main men – helped to sell Ocean's Eleven (1960).*

ABOVE *Stars in the old days had to be glamorous above all else. Here Stewart Granger and Elizabeth Taylor do their best to match up.*

THE SCREEN GODDESSES

There have been many contenders for the status of screen goddess. To qualify, the star must have become immensely popular with millions of people, have signified something transcendental to her fans, have conquered the medium of film through her beauty, charisma and talent, and have acquired a cult status either before or after her death. Every movie fan would have a different short-list, so I offer these first four stars very tentatively as contenders for the title.

MARY PICKFORD (1893–1979)

Pickford was known as "America's Sweetheart" during the heyday of silent movies. Her forte was a child-like demureness allied to an all-American steeliness, for beneath her girlish locks was the mind of an astute businesswoman who knew her own market-worth in the industry that made her world-famous. Sam

Goldwyn stated that it took longer to frame one of Pickford's contracts than it did to shoot her movies. With Charlie Chaplin, D.W. Griffith and Douglas Fairbanks, to whom she was married, she was one of the co-founders of United Artists in 1919.

Pickford earned mega-bucks even by today's standards, Paramount paying her $675,000 a year at one time. A succession of "childwoman" parts in movies such as *The Little Princess*, *Rebecca of Sunnybrook Farm*, *Pollyanna* and *Tess of the Storm Country* gave her immense clout with her bosses. Other movies she made included *Little Lord Fauntleroy*, *Dorothy Vernon of Haddon Hall*, *Little Annie Rooney* and *My Best Girl*. By the time sound arrived in Hollywood she was in her mid-30s; she could no longer play ingenues and she was so identified with the silents that there was clearly no future for her. However, she stayed active in the business through United Artists and lived on until 1979. Pickford lived out the American Dream, reaching dizzying heights of popular and financial success. Unlike many other Hollywood luminaries, however, she was a survivor. "Rebecca of Sunnybrook Farm" was no pushover.

GRETA GARBO (1905–90)

Garbo was born Greta Gustafsson in Stockholm in 1905. Her early Swedish films show her as an unremarkable young woman, more tomboyish than alluring. But her early silent movies in America – *The Torrent*, *The Temptress* and *Flesh and the Devil* –

ABOVE *Mary Pickford starred in the sentimental drama* Secrets (1933). *Dubbed "America's Sweetheart", she married Douglas Fairbanks.*

ABOVE *MGM believed in "classy" product. Their idea of this was to adapt Tolstoy's* Anna Karenina *in the 1927 picture* Love *and cast glamorous stars Greta Garbo and John Gilbert. Garbo and Gilbert enjoyed their off-screen affair but Garbo ended it in 1929.*

established her as a woman men would die for, or at least commit adultery with.

In the talkies she went for a more realistic image with *Anna Christie* and *Susan Lenox (Her Fall and Rise)*, then resorted to ethereal parts such as *Queen Christina* and *Camille*. She lost her heart to John Barrymore in *Grand Hotel* and to Fredric March in *Anna Karenina*, but no male co-star was really good enough for her, according to her admirers. Her fans adored her mixture of spirituality and sensuality. She also had an androgynous quality that meant she had a wider appeal than more overtly heterosexual stars. William Daniels was her favourite cameraman and he made sure, as she

ABOVE *Garbo was presented as the ultimate symbol of female beauty and mystery in romantic melodramas such as* Camille, *which co-starred Robert Taylor. Garbo played the doomed courtesan Marguerite Gautier.*

ABOVE *Garbo made* A Woman of Affairs *with former silent-screen star John Gilbert in 1929. Despite Garbo's support, Gilbert's career vanished with the coming of sound because he had a high-pitched voice.*

herself did, that the lighting and the poses she struck were always kind to her.

But could she act? The jury is still out on that one. Sometimes she is very bad indeed (witness her part as the ballerina in *Grand Hotel*) but to Garbo fanatics, questions about her acting skills are totally irrelevant. They worship her as a transcendent symbol of beauty and of the human spirit, as an embodiment of love – albeit a bisexual love.

The hard fact was that Garbo was always much more popular in Europe than in the USA, so when America entered World War II and the European markets for US films were cut off, the studios were none too keen to make more films with her, especially as her last, *Two-Faced Woman*, had been a flop. Her famous "I want to be alone" retirement line may be misleading; her screen career was almost certainly in serious decline by then. However, that is doubtless sacrilege to the many millions of fans who, despite her death in 1990, will go on worshipping at her shrine.

MARLENE DIETRICH (1901–92)

Dietrich was another screen goddess with an androgynous appeal. Like Garbo, she was European-born – in Berlin in 1901. Her first big hit was in the German movie *The Blue Angel*. Director Josef Von Sternberg also directed her first American film, *Morocco* (1930), in which she starred with Gary Cooper. Von Sternberg was a key figure in Dietrich's Hollywood career, directing her in *Dishonored, Shanghai Express, Blonde Venus, The Scarlet Empress* and *The Devil is a Woman*. In all these movies Dietrich played the vamp, the imperious mistress for

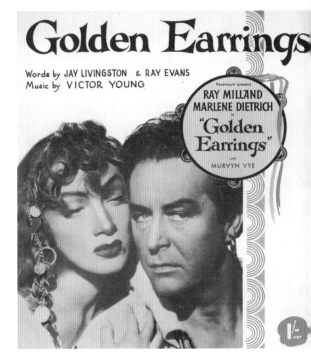

ABOVE *Marlene Dietrich was meant to be exotic and mysterious, so in* Golden Earrings *she played a romantic gypsy.*

whom men ruined themselves. Von Sternberg's wife certainly thought Dietrich played that part in real life because she served a writ on Dietrich accusing her of alienating her husband's affections.

After Von Sternberg's professional relationship with Dietrich ended, her career was never quite the same. Indeed, she was labelled "box-office poison" for a time, before movies such as *Destry Rides Again, Rancho Notorious* and *Witness for the Prosecution* partly revived her film career. Finally, in the 1950s, and in her own 50s, she embarked on an international cabaret career which brought her new fans and fame.

For those who adored Dietrich, there was no one like her. For those who found her eminently resistible, it was puzzling why she won herself such cult status. Dietrich was never an acting talent; what she had was a certain bisexual appeal, an icy beauty, an exotic style and a ravenous ego that saw to it that she was shown on the silver screen in as flattering a light as possible.

MARILYN MONROE
(1926–62)

More words have been written about Monroe than any other movie star. A mixture of fantasy, fact, legend and downright fabrication make up the Monroe legend; indeed, "Marilyn Monroe" is now an industry even 40 years after her death. Fans of "Norma Jean" collect everything associated with her, writers never tire of writing about her and her movies are still very popular. Along with James Dean, she is the Hollywood star who has provoked and continues to provoke the most intense cult worship.

Born in Los Angeles in 1926, Norma Jean Mortenson had a paranoid schizophrenic mother, no father, various unbalanced relatives and several foster homes. These childhood experiences must have contributed hugely to her later instabilities and her search for that solid parent figure, particularly the male parent, that led her into disastrous relationships and marriages with older men. The hardships she endured undoubtedly also gave her the drive to succeed, to get herself out of this morass of abuse and poverty.

To do this, Monroe was forced to exploit her looks: her (dyed) blonde hair, her appealing face and her voluptuous body. Evidence has piled up that her early film career was greatly helped by various elderly gentlemen in the movie business. Monroe is quoted as saying she spent a lot of time on her knees in her early starlet days. Her first significant role was in *The Asphalt Jungle*, directed by John Huston, in which she played

OPPOSITE *Monroe looks sad in her role in* Bus Stop *(1956). Her off-screen life had rare spells of happiness and ended in a mysterious death. This has only added to her mystique.*

elderly Louis Calhern's mistress. She looked beautiful and she was also rather touching in this small part.

Undoubtedly Monroe had a quality when she was on screen. She could play dumb blonde parts with an instinctive grasp of comedy, as in *How to Marry a Millionaire*, *Gentlemen Prefer Blondes*, *The Seven Year Itch* and *Some Like it Hot*. Male viewers were attracted by her sexuality but felt unchallenged by her "little girl" voice and general helplessness; men were allowed to be attracted to her and be protective as well. Because she played powerless young women, this angered the more feminist of cinema-goers, who dismissed her as a middle-aged man's fantasy object, but many women liked her because of her vulnerability.

Marriages to James Dougherty, baseball star Joe DiMaggio and playwright Arthur Miller all failed. Attracted to the mixture of power and sex that John Kennedy exuded, Monroe had an affair with the president, who seemingly asked brother Bobby to take care of her when she started to get "troublesome". Bobby himself had an affair with her and then the scenario becomes

ABOVE *Marilyn Monroe had a big hit with* Some Like it Hot *(1959), but the way she was represented in that Billy Wilder comedy undoubtedly contributed to the tensions that arose during filming.*

blurred. Whether Monroe's death through an overdose of barbiturates was an accident, suicide or murder has not yet been finally established. Certainly, what we do know about the end of her life exposes the seamier side of Hollywood's connections with power politics.

Monroe is often written about as a victim figure, and undoubtedly she was treated shabbily at times. But she was a determined woman, driven by her need to make up for childhood deprivations of material and emotional security. Finally, she never achieved that security because she was never allowed, in the years of her fame, to be herself. The men who became involved with her went to bed with Marilyn Monroe but made sure they never woke up with Norma Jean Mortenson. Perhaps what fans worship about Monroe is the ordinary Norma Jean they sense under the glamorous Marilyn exterior.

LEFT *Many people's idea of a contemporary, glamorous star is Julia Roberts, here with Patrick Bergin in* Sleeping with the Enemy *(1991).*

JULIA ROBERTS (b. 1967)

Roberts is many people's idea of a glamorous leading lady. Certainly, she is currently a top box-office star. For some of us, this is a very puzzling phenomenon. Whereas her many fans see her as a beautiful and talented star, others wonder exactly why this actress with such limited talents and average looks has reached such a position in the cinema hierarchy. She first came to prominence in the appalling *Pretty Woman* (1990), a piece of Hollywood fluff that was decidedly unappealing. *Sleeping with the Enemy* and *Flatliners* did her career no harm, while the lachrymose *Dying Young* positively enhanced it. *My Best Friend's Wedding* and *Notting Hill* were the type of light and forgettable comedies that endear her to her adoring audience. Amazingly, her role in *Erin Brockovich* won her the Best Actress Oscar, which says more about the judgement of the members of the Academy than her acting abilities.

NICOLE KIDMAN (b. 1967)

Born in Hawaii and raised in Australia, Kidman has acquired major star status within a relatively short time. *Dead Calm* (1989) was the first movie she was really noticed in, and then *Flirting* and *Far and Away* consolidated her status. The 1995 *To Die For*, in which she played an ambitious television weather girl, showed she was more than just a glamorous leading lady, and the underrated *The Portrait of a Lady* proved she could tackle serious roles. She fared better in Kubrick's *Eyes Wide Shut* than her husband at the time, Tom Cruise, and she followed this up with a major success in *Moulin Rouge*. *The Others* was a small-scale thriller which found an audience, then she won her first Oscar for her portrayal of Virginia Woolf in *The Hours*. In between movies, she returns to the theatre and takes on more demanding roles than the cinema can give her. The test for Kidman as a movie star is whether she can jump over the age barrier that Hollywood erects to frustrate actresses.

ABOVE *Nicole Kidman showed she was more than a glamorous movie star in films such as* To Die For *(1995) and* The Hours *(2002), for which she won the Best Actress Oscar.*

THE ROMANTIC HEROES

Romantic heroes or male heart-throbs – call them what you will – there have been numerous major stars who were famous for their combination of good looks, devil-may-care screen personas and their on-screen womanizing. Here is a short list of seven.

RUDOLPH VALENTINO (1895–1926)

Valentino was the screen's first "Great Lover", a title that caused him problems both with other men and his wives. He danced a tango in *The Four Horsemen of the Apocalypse* (1921) and set female pulses racing. His preposterous role in *The Sheik*, a desert chieftain with propensities towards rape, found an ecstatic audience. Marital difficulties with actress Jean Acker and designer Natasha Rambova

and problems with Paramount put a great deal of pressure on the superstar, as did press insinuations of bisexuality. He died of a ruptured appendix in 1926 at the age of 31. The scenes of extravagant mourning at his funeral have passed into Hollywood legend. The Valentino phenomenon is evidence of the power of the screen image over a mass audience hungry for erotic fantasy.

CLARK GABLE (1901–60)

Gable was known as "The King of Hollywood". He was certainly the most popular male star of the late 1930s and 40s. His most famous role was Rhett Butler in *Gone with the Wind*. He was popular with men because he was an uncomplicated action hero and did not make a big deal about his success with the ladies. Women liked him for his sexuality, his ready charm and his easy-going persona. He won an Oscar for *It Happened One Night* but was never perceived as a great screen

ABOVE *Ronald Colman was an English actor who played romantic heroes initially in the silents, then very successfully in the sound era. Sidney Carton in the 1935 version of Dickens's* A Tale of Two Cities *was one of Colman's most famous roles.*

ABOVE *Rudolph Valentino was one of the biggest stars of the silent era. His sudden death at a young age set off a worldwide surge of grief, and several women reportedly committed suicide because of their sense of loss. His appeal has certainly dated.*

ABOVE *Clark Gable did not get on well with Vivien Leigh, his co-star in* Gone with the Wind. *He married his third wife, Carole Lombard, in the midst of filming this picture in 1939.*

actor, although he was praised for his performance in his final film with Marilyn Monroe, *The Misfits*. He was married to Carole Lombard for a few years before she died in an air crash in 1942. In 1961, 12 days after filming ended on *The Misfits*, Gable died of a heart attack, probably brought on by the action scenes he had insisted on doing himself in the movie. Perhaps it was a case of Gable's screen image catching up with the man.

ERROL FLYNN (1909–59)

The greatest of the swashbuckling stars, Flynn was as famous for his off-screen antics as his celluloid heroics. Determinedly self-destructive, Flynn drank his health and wealth away and died in 1959 at the age of 50. At his peak in the 1930s and early 40s, he was very big at the box office in movies such as *Captain Blood*, *The Charge of the Light Brigade*, *The Sea Hawk*, *They Died with Their Boots On*

and *The Private Lives of Elizabeth and Essex*. By the 1950s his alcoholism had ruined his outstanding good looks and he was reduced to starring with Anna Neagle in film versions of *Lilacs in the Spring* and *King's Rhapsody*. He played a drunk in *The Sun Also Rises* and *Too Much Too Soon* (as John Barrymore), but the end was near. His body finally gave out in a Vancouver hotel when he died of a heart attack. Since his death, bizarre rumours have linked him with Nazi espionage and the IRA. Flynn, even in death, is seldom far from a headline.

ROBERT REDFORD (b. 1937)

Redford is unlike Valentino, Gable and Flynn in that he is not predominantly an action hero. However, he has become a symbol of male beauty whether he likes it or not. His roles in *Butch Cassidy and the Sundance Kid*, *The Candidate*, *The Way We Were*, *The Sting*, *All the President's Men*

ABOVE Robert Redford as Bob Woodward of Woodward and Bernstein, the investigative reporters who broke the Watergate story, in Alan J. Pakula's All the President's Men.

and *The Natural* have made him a major star, albeit not in the tradition of Gable. Redford has no great range as an actor. He tends to play the honest guy trying to make his way in the world in as honourable a manner as he can. In the process, however, he always looks impossibly handsome in the tradition of Hollywood romantic heroes. However, he is much more than a handsome leading man, as his direction of *Ordinary People*, *A River Runs Through It*, *Quiz Show* and *The Horse Whisperer* clearly shows. Other notable movies he has acted in include *Jeremiah Johnson* (1972), *The Great Gatsby* (1974), *Three Days of the Condor* (1975), *Brubaker* (1980), *Out of Africa* (1985), *Up Close and Personal* (1996) and *Spy Game* (2001).

"THEY THROW THAT WORD 'STAR' AT YOU LOOSELY AND THEY TAKE IT AWAY EQUALLY LOOSELY. YOU TAKE THE RESPONSIBILITY FOR THEIR LOUSY MOVIE, THAT'S WHAT THAT MEANS."
ROBERT REDFORD

GEORGE CLOONEY (b. 1961)

Clooney graduated to the cinema from the television series *ER* and is now a major box-office star. He began to be really noticed when he made *From Dusk Till Dawn*, *One Fine Day* and *Batman and Robin*. He can play action heroes as in *Three Kings* and *The Perfect Storm*, but his performances are usually leavened with a good measure of humour and self-deprecation. He

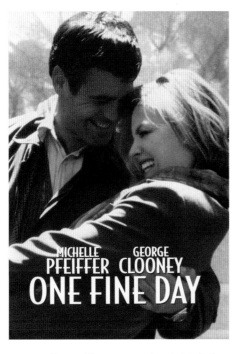

ABOVE *George Clooney starred with Michelle Pfeiffer in the romantic comedy* One Fine Day.

showed his comic talent in the Coen Brothers' *O Brother, Where Art Thou?*, which was a welcome change of style for him, and *Intolerable Cruelty*. However, the remake of *Ocean's Eleven* and its sequel *Ocean's Twelve* reminded us how mainstream he is. He is likely to have real lasting power as a major star. He has turned his hand to producing, and directed *Confessions of a Dangerous Mind*.

TOM CRUISE (b. 1962)

After appearing in "youth pics" such as *Taps*, *All the Right Moves* and *The Outsiders*, Cruise hit the big time with *Top Gun*, a mindless piece of macho nonsense. Cruise exudes a kind of rather smug, locker-room masculinity, but this seems to appeal to a large

proportion of the female audience. *The Color of Money*, *Cocktail*, *Rain Man* and *Born on the Fourth of July* further enhanced his career. The *Mission: Impossible* movies made him a fortune but only added to the list of no-brainers he has appeared in. He tried something more ambitious with Kubrick's final movie, *Eyes Wide Shut*, in which he appeared with his then-wife, Nicole Kidman, but he failed to convince in a disappointing film. He shed his cocky college jock persona and began growing up as an actor around the time he turned 40, with films such as *Vanilla Sky*, *The Last Samurai* and *Collateral*.

BEN AFFLECK (b. 1972)

The fact is that Affleck has attained major box-office status in recent years, so he must appeal to a lot of people. He exudes a kind of smugness on screen, however, that is un-appealing to some. He had a hit with the amusing *Chasing Amy* and followed that up with *Good Will Hunting*, which he co-wrote with his friend, Matt Damon. His career has survived a succession of

ABOVE *Tom Cruise played agent Ethan Hunt in the first of the* Mission Impossible *movies that he starred in. Here he comes to grips with the bad guy, played by Jean Reno.*

awful movies, the worst of which was *Pearl Harbor* (2001), a truly authentic turkey that reached ludicrous levels of badness. Affleck's name never seems to be far from the gossip columns and he is one of those Hollywood actors who seem to settle for being more Hollywood than actor.

BELOW *Leonardo DiCaprio became a superstar wooing Kate Winslet in* Titanic *(1997).*

15

THE SENSITIVE ANTI-HEROES

In the 1950s there appeared a new kind of male star: the intuitive, almost feminized hero. Usually anti-authoritarian in stance, these stars grew out of the naturalistic, "Method" school of acting and the commercial need to give Hollywood's dominant audience in the 1950s – young people of between 16 and 25 – stars they could identify with.

MONTGOMERY CLIFT (1920–66)

Clift was the first of the sensitive, emotional actors to make it as a major star. His mumbling, hesitant style suited his roles in *A Place in the Sun, The Heiress, I Confess, From Here to Eternity, The Young Lions, Suddenly Last Summer* and *The Misfits*. His spectacular good looks did not harm his career either,

but a serious car smash in 1957 altered his appearance and probably eventually shortened his life. Insecure in his private life and uncertain about his sexual identity, he resorted to drink and drugs and died prematurely at the age of 46. Clift influenced other young stars of the 1950s and was undoubtedly, in his own way, a powerful screen presence.

JAMES DEAN (1931–55)

An enormous worldwide cult has grown around James Dean which, almost 50 years after his death at the age of 24, shows no sign of dying out. Like Monroe, he is still big business. People who have never seen his films buy posters and other memorabilia of him because he represents youth, rebellion and charisma.

In real life, Dean rebelled against the straitjacket that Hollywood tried to put him into; he would not conform to the image-makers' idea of what a Hollywood star should be, and in this he was just like his great hero, Marlon Brando. Dean's style is similar to Brando's except it is even more mannered, boyish and self-conscious. But he had tremendous screen presence, and an ability to dominate the screen space and force the audience to look at him.

All actors are narcissistic, but Dean seemed to have narcissism to excess. The need to display himself and his emotions on screen was

BELOW *Method actor Montgomery Clift starred with Eve Marie Saint in the Civil War epic* Raintree County (1957).

LEFT *"You're tearing me apart!" screams Dean at his father. Sal Mineo played another teenager with extreme angst in the 1955* Rebel Without a Cause.

BELOW *James Dean in a convincing role as Jet Rink with co-star Elizabeth Taylor, and squaring up to Rock Hudson in* Giant *(1956), the last movie Dean completed before his death in a car accident.*

overwhelming, whatever he might have said about remaining a private person. But he did acknowledge that acting was about an actor's inner fantasies: "My neuroticism manifests itself in the dramatic. Why do most actors act? To express the fantasies in which they have involved themselves." Dean's talent lay in his power to involve mass audiences in those inner fantasies.

He had made only three major films by the time of his death: *East of Eden* and *Rebel Without a Cause* (both 1955) and *Giant* (1956). In *East of Eden* he played Cal Trask, the moody, disaffected son of Adam Trask, played by Raymond Massey.

Elia Kazan directed the movie and has written about how Dean's improvisatory style irritated Massey, who was of the old school of actors, believing in knowing your lines and your moves. In one famous scene in the movie, Dean throws his arms around Massey's neck, imploring him to say that he (his father) loves him. This had not been rehearsed and completely threw Massey, although the scene as it was shot remains in the film. Kazan admits that he used the antagonism between Dean and Massey to generate on-screen tension – in fact, he surreptitiously encouraged it between the two stars. *Rebel Without a Cause* had Dean as a

disturbed high-school teenager on the verge of becoming a fully developed teenage delinquent – largely because of the lack of love and stability in his home life. Although Natalie Wood and Sal Mineo form a kind of substitute family, Dean completely dominates. Nicholas Ray, the director, privileged him by allowing him to steal scenes and placing him in the dominating space on the screen. Dean in this persona, and in his playing of Cal Trask, seemed to encapsulate a rebellious attitude among America's youth that was to boil over into the mass protests of the 1960s.

Giant was his last film (only *East of Eden* had been released by the time of his death). In it he co-starred with Rock Hudson and Elizabeth Taylor, playing another outsider part: Jet Rink, the penniless orphan who becomes an oil millionaire. His hesitant style suited the young Jet Rink, but when he had to age in the latter parts of the movie, his lack of technique showed through and his acting is almost amateurish.

On September 30, 1955, Dean was killed while driving his Porsche along a Californian highway. He died a death that fed the legend of the rebel who lived for kicks, speed and fighting adult hypocrisy and conformity. The myths grew around him: was he homosexual or bisexual? Was his death an accident or was he murdered by proxy by Rock Hudson, a one-time lover? Truth never mixes well with legend, so it is unlikely we will ever know the real James Dean. The only Dean that really counts is the one who appeared in those three films, but the cultists want much more than that from this icon of the cinema. The Dean legend represents something meaningful to millions of people, and shows no sign of disappearing from our culture.

17

ABOVE *Paul Newman and Robert Redford teamed up very successfully as conmen in* The Sting (1970), *which was a box-office hit.*

PAUL NEWMAN (b. 1925)

At the beginning of his career Paul Newman was accused of copying Brando, but he went on to become a superstar in his own right. His first success was playing an inarticulate boxer in *Somebody Up There Likes Me*, and he followed that by playing Billy the Kid in Arthur Penn's *The Left-Handed Gun*, a western that aimed to demythologize cowboy legends. Newman's sensitive style suited his roles in *Cat on a Hot Tin Roof* and *The Hustler*, but was less successful in comedies such as *Lady L* and *The Secret War of Harry Frigg*.

Of the new breed of actor, Newman was always more macho than the rest, notably in *Hud*, *Hombre* and *Cool Hand Luke*. He had great success in the 1970s with *Butch Cassidy and the Sundance Kid* and *The Sting*. He also turned to directing, including directing his wife Joanne Woodward in *Rachel Rachel*.

His pursuits in real life include liberal politics, and these liberal sentiments are reflected in some of his movies: *WUSA*, *Absence of Malice* and *The Verdict*. He has accepted the aging process gracefully and played roles accordingly: in *Harry and Son*, *The Color of Money*, *Blaze*, *The Hudsucker Proxy*, *Nobody's Fool* and *Road to Perdition*. He is quoted as being sick of morons coming up to him and asking him to remove his dark glasses so they can see his steely blue eyes. He has always fought against being stereotyped as a romantic leading man.

DUSTIN HOFFMAN (b. 1937)

Hoffmann became a star with his role as an unsure young man eaten up by Mrs Robinson in *The Graduate* (1967). Other notable parts have been in *Midnight Cowboy*, *Little Big Man*, *Kramer vs Kramer*, *Tootsie* and *Rain Man*. Hoffman obviously prides himself on the range of roles he has attempted; he has also appeared in overtly violent movies (*Straw Dogs*, *Papillon* and *Marathon Man*), but he basically always plays the decent individual with doubts and inadequacies struggling against a cruel and indifferent world. He returns to the stage from time to time and appeared in the film version of David Mamet's play *American Buffalo*. In the late 1980s and 90s he made some poor films such as *Family Business*, *Outbreak* and *Sphere*. He has a reputation for being "difficult", but that probably arises

ABOVE *Dustin Hoffmann had a major success playing the character of Ratso in John Schlesinger's movie about New York low life,* Midnight Cowboy (1969).

from his obsession with getting things right on screen. During the making of *Marathon Man* he so exasperated Laurence Olivier with his detailed Method-style preparation for a scene that Olivier finally declared, "Why don't you just try acting?"

BELOW *Sean Penn and Michael J. Fox starred in the Vietnam movie* Casualties of War, *directed by Brian De Palma.*

ABOVE *Matt Damon has proved himself an actor of some depth in movies such as* Good Will Hunting *and* The Talented Mr Ripley.

ABOVE *Matthew Broderick as he appeared in* Biloxi Blues. *Broderick plays contemporary good guys and has a likeable screen presence.*

ABOVE *Johnny Depp as the legendary worst director of all time, Ed Wood, in the 1994 movie of the same name directed by Tim Burton.*

JOHN CUSACK (b. 1966)

Cusack seems to care more than most Hollywood actors about the roles he is willing to take on. As a rule he avoids macho, violent roles and prefers to play ambivalent parts such as his characters in *The Grifters, Grosse Pointe Blank, The Thin Red Line, Being John Malkovich* and *Pushing Tin.* He scored another success in *High Fidelity* (2000). He is definitely one of the more intelligent of the younger breed of Hollywood actors.

SEAN PENN (b. 1960)

Penn was one of the group of young Hollywood actors who graduated in the early 1980s from movies such as *Taps, Fast Times at Ridgemont High, Bad Boys* and *Racing with the Moon* to more adult roles. He occasionally plays the heavy as in De Palma's *Casualties of War,* or self-destructive hedonists as in *Carlito's Way.* He was memorable in *Dead Man Walking* and *Hurly Burly,* and played against type as a jazz guitarist in *Sweet and Lowdown.* He has directed three movies: *The Indian Runner, The Crossing Guard* and *The Pledge.* His public pronouncements often come over as arrogant, but the man has talent. His role as a mentally deficient father in *I am Sam* was a major error but he bounced back with an Oscar-winning role in Eastwood's *Mystic River,* and a powerful performance in *21 Grams.*

MATT DAMON (b. 1970)

Damon is a talented actor of intelligence and versatility. He came to the fore with *Good Will Hunting,* for which he wrote the screenplay. He then appeared in *Saving Private Ryan* and memorably in *The Talented Mr Ripley.* It is apt that Redford chose Damon to star in *The Legend of Bagger Vance,* the movie about golf that Redford directed in 2000; Damon does not have the young Redford's matinée idol looks, but he has something of the same screen presence about him, which helped to make his role as a CIA operative in the *Bourne* films so successful. Unlike many of his contemporaries, Damon seems willing to take on unglamorous roles, and his career should continue to prosper.

MATTHEW BRODERICK (b. 1962)

Broderick came to the fore with the 1986 hit *Ferris Bueller's Day Off.* He followed that up with *Biloxi Blues* and *Glory.* He starred opposite Brando in *The Freshman* and Jim Carrey in *The Cable Guy.* His niche part is the decent guy facing life's problems with a puzzled but honourable attitude.

BRAD PITT (b. 1963)

Fans of the television series *Dallas* will probably remember Pitt appearing in a few episodes, but it was with his part in *Thelma and Louise* that he really came to prominence. Redford chose him to play the self-destructive brother in *A River Runs Through It,* then he played a psychotic killer in *Kalifornia.* Appearing in *True Romance* helped to consolidate his growing cult status and then *Legends of the Fall, Seven, Twelve Monkeys* and *Sleepers* all proved beneficial to his career. He was major box-office, but that did not prevent the failure of *Meet Joe Black* and *Seven Years in Tibet.* *Fight Club, Snatch* and *Troy* provided more macho roles, while the *Ocean's* films failed to test him as an actor.

BELOW *Brad Pitt has shown he can act in Redford's* A River Runs Through It *and* Legends of the Fall.

19

THE COMEDY STARS

LEFT *Charlie Chaplin in his classic "Chaplin" persona in* The Gold Rush *(1925): the bowler hat, the cane and the baggy trousers.*

was a cinematic phenomenon, and however opinions diverge about his worth as a performer and director, his fame illustrates how cinema is a worldwide form of communication that crosses barriers of language and culture.

W.C. FIELDS (1879–1946)

Fields played misogynistic braggarts and cheats, who viewed the world cynically and through a whisky bottle. He communicated his dislike for women and children in his "act", which almost certainly owed a great deal to the real-life Fields. His comic appearance with that bulbous, whisky-red nose meant that he could never play for pathos although,

ABOVE *Charlie Chaplin starred with his then-wife Paulette Goddard in* The Great Dictator *(1940), a satire on Hitler. Chaplin's left-wing political views eventually brought him into hot water with the US authorities, and his American passport was withdrawn in the 1950s.*

CHARLIE CHAPLIN (1889–1977)

The little man with the baggy pants and bowler hat became one of the icons of the cinema. However, opinions divide over Chaplin, and I find myself having to admit that I find his movies unfunny. They are also spoiled by a gross sentimentality. But there is no denying Chaplin's fame and popularity. Early movies such as *The Tramp, The Pawnshop* and *Easy Street* established him as a major star and *The Kid, The Gold Rush, The Circus* and *City Lights* are perceived as masterpieces by Chaplin fans. In the 1930s *Modern Times* and *The Great Dictator* showed Chaplin's brand of sentimental liberal politicizing, and it was this aspect of his work that gave ammunition to reactionaries in America who demanded that his passport be withdrawn until he could prove his "moral worth".

Monsieur Verdoux (1947), perhaps Chaplin's best film, was followed by *Limelight* (1952), *A King in New York* (1957) and *A Countess from Hong Kong* (1967). Finally, Hollywood "forgave" Chaplin and awarded him a special Oscar in 1972. "Charlie Chaplin"

ABOVE *W.C. Fields played the Great McGonigle in* The Old Fashioned Way *(1934).*

unlike Chaplin, he was temperamentally unwilling to milk tears anyway. His biggest successes were *The Old Fashioned Way, It's a Gift, David Copperfield* (as Mr Micawber), *Poppy, You Can't Cheat an Honest Man, My Little Chickadee, The Bank Dick* and *Never Give a Sucker an Even Break.* His alcoholism caught up with him on Christmas Day, 1946.

RIGHT *W.C. Fields was the ultimate cynical funny man in* Never Give a Sucker an Even Break.

LEFT *Laurel and Hardy are for many fans the greatest of the movie clowns. Indeed, their fans are among the most loyal of all in the movie world, despite the fact that the duo ceased making movies almost half a century ago.*

GROUCHO MARX (1890–1977)

The only one of the Marx Brothers really to count, it was Groucho who gave the brothers class and wit in movies such as *Animal Crackers, Monkey Business, Horse Feathers, Duck Soup, A Night at the Opera, A Day at the Races* and *Room Service.* His best partner in comedy was the mountainous matron, Margaret Dumont, whom Groucho systematically insulted. Irretrievably sexist, Groucho still managed to be funny and sharp. His trademarks were a painted-on moustache, heavy eyebrows, steel-rimmed spectacles, a cigar and a mad, crouching walk. He was a verbal and physical clown whose humour depended on elaborate wordplay and puns. Perhaps it was this aspect of his clowning that gained him intellectual fans, including T.S. Eliot, with whom he conducted a long correspondence: "Marry me and I'll never look at another horse!"

BOB HOPE (1903–2003)

At the peak of his career Bob Hope was among the biggest box-office stars, especially in the series of *Road* movies he made with Bing Crosby.

Paramount made a mint out of these (which included *Road to Singapore, Road to Zanzibar, Road to Morocco, Road to Utopia*). Other Hope hits were *The Cat and the Canary, The Ghost Breakers, My Favorite Blonde, Monsieur Beaucaire, The Paleface* and *The Lemon Drop Kid.*

His screen persona was based on a cowardly and rather narcissistic nincompoop, always falling for Crosby's streetwise ruses and seldom getting the girl.

As his films deteriorated in the late 1950s and 60s, he turned more and more to television. He also became extremely reactionary in his politics and was associated with jingoistic tours of Vietnam. But Hope was also something of a national institution and the resident White House clown.

ABOVE *Bob Hope was one of the biggest stars of the 1940s and 50s. Here he plays his usual coward in the spoof western Alias Jesse James (1959).*

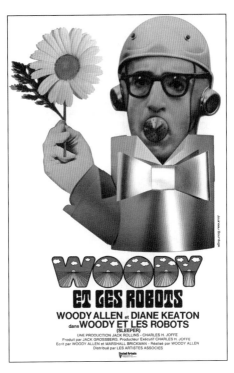

ABOVE *Sleeper (1973) is Woody Allen's spoof sci-fi movie. Allen is still churning out a movie a year, but they now have a more tired feel to them.*

WOODY ALLEN (b. 1935)

Allen could have appeared in the section on directors because he has directed and written most of his most important films. However, he is best known in the public mind as a performer in worldly New York comedies such as *Play It Again, Sam, Annie Hall, Manhattan, Stardust Memories, Broadway Danny Rose, The Purple Rose of Cairo* and *Radio Days*. In the 1990s he directed *Husbands and Wives, Manhattan Murder Mystery, Bullets Over Broadway, Mighty Aphrodite, Everyone Says I Love You, Deconstructing Harry, Celebrity* and *Sweet and Lowdown*. Allen keeps making movies but even his most ardent fans must detect a falling away in quality. This was confirmed by the feeble *Small Time Crooks* (2000).

For his humour he leans heavily on his Jewish background and his show-business career. His obsessions are death, sex, potency, his looks and his Jewishness. Allen started in stand-up comedy and those origins are reflected in the one-liners that pepper his scripts. There is a knowing, self-conscious quality to the writing that flatters the audience who congratulate themselves on picking up the Freudian or cultural references. He has also directed "serious" movies such as *Interiors* and *September*, which are very much influenced by his cinematic hero, Swedish director Ingmar Bergman.

Woody Allen divides people like few other performers: if you are an Allen fan, you tend to be a devotee who becomes boring after a while recounting favourite bits from the movies; if you're not, you can't see what all the fuss is about. His view of life? "I don't believe in an after-life, but I'm bringing along a change of underwear."

STEVE MARTIN (b. 1945)

Graduating from stand-up comedy and television's *Saturday Night Live*, Martin did not take long to establish himself as one of Hollywood's top comic actors. *The Jerk* (1979) featured one of his comic personas, the hopeless naive adrift in a knowing world. *Dead Men Don't Wear Plaid* was a clever parody of detective *film noir* and

ABOVE *Dean Martin and Jerry Lewis formed a highly successful comedy team in the 1940s and 50s before an acrimonious split. Thereafter Lewis's career spiralled downwards, whilst Martin's zoomed upwards.*

BELOW *The Secret Life of Walter Mitty is one of Danny Kaye's most enduringly popular movies. Kaye was a great favourite on screen for many years – an inspired clown who too often fell back on pathos in his later years.*

23

STEVE MARTIN, CHIRURGIEN DE RENOMMÉE MONDIALE, A MIS AU POINT LA BOÎTE CRANIENNE A VIS POUR LES OPÉRATIONS DU CERVEAU. AYEZ CONFIANCE!

ABOVE Steve Martin had a huge success with The Man with Two Brains *(1983), a story about a world-famous surgeon who invented screw-top, zip-lock brain surgery.*

Roxanne a reworking of *Cyrano de Bergerac*. He starred with Michael Caine in *Dirty Rotten Scoundrels* as a con man. But not all of Martin's choices of work have been wise: why remake the 1950 *Father of the Bride* with himself in the Spencer Tracy role and then follow it up with a feeble sequel? Martin is, however, an actor who can play "serious", as he showed in *Grand Canyon* and *The Spanish Prisoner*. *Bowfinger* marked a return to comic form, but a remake of the Jack Lemmon movie *The Out-of-Towners* smacked of desperation.

JIM CARREY (b. 1962)

A Canadian, Carrey is "funny in his bones", but too often the movies he makes fail to exploit his undoubted talents. He made his breakthrough with *Ace Ventura: Pet Detective* (1994), and followed that with *The Mask* and the gross-out comedy *Dumb and Dumber*. His humour is too often scatological and tends to the juvenile, which is a pity because he is a genuinely funny guy. He made a second *Ace Ventura* movie, *When Nature Calls* and then tried a change of style

and pace in *The Cable Guy*, in which he played a sinister television installer who gradually impacts big time on a customer's life. In that movie and perhaps also in *Liar, Liar* and *The Truman Show*, Carrey is more than hinting at the latent aggression that many comedians have towards their potential audiences. He received high praise for his performances in *The Truman Show* and *Eternal Sunshine of the Spotless Mind*, indicating that he is capable of playing straight roles as well as being a natural clown.

MIKE MYERS (b. 1963)

Myers, like Jim Carrey, is a Canadian (perhaps you need a well-developed sense of humour to live in Canada). He too emerged from the US television show *Saturday Night Live*, in which he and Dana Carvey created *Wayne's World*, a very knowing spoof of teen rock programmes. They transferred that show to the big screen in 1992 and it was a gigantic hit. On the back of that success, he made *So I Married an Axe Murderer* and then inevitably *Wayne's World 2*. However, Myers really hit the big time with the first *Austin Powers* movie in 1997. This spoof of James Bond and other 1960s culture icons was a surprise megahit. The first movie was very knowing and relatively amusing, but the later sequels were feeble in comparison. In Hollywood, the danger is that you

ABOVE Jim Carrey's career took off with the Ace Ventura *movies. He has since proved himself a competent actor in movies such as* The Truman Show *(1998) and* Eternal Sunshine of the Spotless Mind *(2004).*

can sometimes be too successful so that you go on churning out what has made you hugely popular in the first place – and that usually spells artistic death. If Myers wants to exploit his comic talents – and he is a funny man – then he will have to leave *Austin Powers* behind him and try to expand his comic range.

BELOW Mike Myers reached new heights with the Austin Powers *movies. A talented man, Myers has to beware of pandering to easy laughs and the lowest common denominator.*

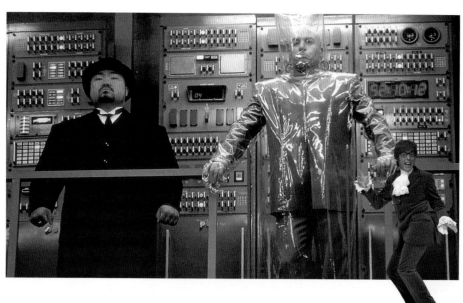

24

THE GLAMOUR QUEENS

In the heyday of Hollywood, female stars usually had to conform to a stereotyped image of female beauty as defined by men. Hopefully, the pressure on contemporary actresses to present a manufactured glamour image is now less intense – witness stars such as Kathleen Turner and Glenn Close. In the days of old Hollywood, however, there were many contenders for the role of glamour queen or sex object.

JEAN HARLOW (1911–37)

Harlow is one of the prime candidates for the dubious honour of being the all-time Hollywood victim. She died at the age of 26, after a short but highly successful career playing blondes-on-the-make. Harlow was one of Howard Hughes's "starlets" – in other words, one of his mistresses whose careers he boosted. She had little acting talent but came over on the screen as a brash, vulgar but determined young woman.

She co-starred with Cagney in *The Public Enemy*, then she became the *Platinum Blonde*. MGM bought up her contract and with them she made *Red Dust*, *Dinner at Eight*, *Reckless* and *Saratoga*. Her marriage to Paul Bern, MGM executive, landed her in scandal: Bern, shortly after their marriage, either shot himself because he was impotent or was murdered by a former woman friend. Harlow's frenetic existence came to an end in 1937 when she died of uremic poisoning. Known as the "blonde bombshell", Harlow discovered the hard way – as many other female stars of her type did – that notoriety and stardom have their own price tag. She is sometimes likened to Monroe, but she seldom revealed the vulnerability that was a Monroe trademark. No doubt in real life Harlow had her vulnerable side, but her public image never allowed her to reveal that side of herself. She was hard-boiled right up until her premature end.

ABOVE Jean Harlow in a typically would-be glamorous pose. The actress was the USA's pre-eminent sex symbol in the mid-1930s.

MAE WEST (1892–1980)

Of all the manufactured female sex objects, Mae West was the most self-conscious and processed. Both a sex symbol and a parody of a sex object, West appealed to a wide spectrum of audience. Her forte was the unsubtle double entendre such as "Is that a gun in your pocket or are you just glad to see me?" Lines like that made West notorious and helped give ammunition to the Legion of Decency and other vigilante censorship groups to clamp down on Hollywood licentiousness. She looked like a man in drag, presenting a grossly stereotypical image of what passed for female sexuality. But she knew what she was doing and was no dumb blonde, writing her own scripts and proving herself to be an expert self-publicist and businesswoman. Her films include *She Done Him Wrong* (1933), *I'm No Angel* (1933), *Belle of the Nineties* (1934), *Klondike Annie* (1936) and *My Little Chickadee* (1940). She made a late and disastrous appearance in the dire *Myra Breckinridge* (1970), and died at the age of 88 in 1980.

ABOVE *"Why don't you come up sometime 'n' see me? I'm home every evening." Mae West was, for many, like a male drag queen and had as much sex appeal as a cabbage, but for some time she was portrayed as a sex icon.*

Rita Hayworth
IN
COLUMBIA PICTURES
TONIGHT AND
EVERY NIGHT
WITH JANET BLAIR · LEE BOWMAN

RITA HAYWORTH (1918–87)

Hayworth could be seen as another victim of the Hollywood system. When she said that the years that she was married to Orson Welles were the happiest of her life, Welles replied that, if that was her idea of happiness, what must the rest of her life have been like? But in the 1940s Hayworth became the glamour queen, enduring painful transformations of her appearance to reach the standard of Hollywood glamour that her studio bosses demanded.

Her best films were *Cover Girl*, *Gilda* and *The Lady from Shanghai*, the latter directed by husband Orson Welles who dyed her hair blonde and made her portray a duplicitous femme fatale. In 1949 Hayworth married Prince Aly Khan, a Muslim leader-cum-playboy, but they were divorced in 1953. In the 1950s her most notable films were *Miss Sadie Thompson*, *Salome*, *Pal Joey* and *Separate Tables*. Alzheimer's Disease came to her at the early age of 62; for the last few years of her life she had to be cared for like a baby.

RIGHT *Lana Turner was an actress of extremely limited talent who survived scandal – including being involved in the stabbing of her lover – to be an enduring top star. She starred with top male star Clark Gable in the 1941* Honky Tonk.

LEFT *Rita Hayworth was a manufactured screen beauty who underwent excruciating treatment to fashion her to studio boss Harry Cohn's ideal of female beauty.*

LANA TURNER (1920–95)

Turner was another totally manufactured Hollywood glamour object. Rarely was she ever anything other than wooden in her roles, but she did achieve some credibility as an actress in *The Bad and the Beautiful* and *Imitation of Life*. Earlier films included *Ziegfeld Girl*, *Dr Jekyll and Mr Hyde*, *The Postman Always Rings Twice* and *The Three Musketeers*. Even the legend of her so-called discovery at Schwab's Drugstore on Sunset Boulevard has been exposed as a manufactured myth dreamed up by some cynical agent.

Her early film career prospered with her label as the "Sweater Girl" and she acquired husbands at a rate of knots: seven in all, including Artie Shaw the bandleader, and Lex Barker, one of many screen Tarzans. In 1958 she was involved in a steamy scandal when her 14-year-old daughter

Cinémonde
CINÉVIE-CINÉVOGUE

HEDY LAMARR

ABOVE *Hedy Lamarr was a very beautiful Austrian-born actress who was defined as a star by her stunning looks.*

27

RIGHT *Jane Russell adorns the front cover of a French fan magazine. This was important exposure for the top female stars.*

stabbed to death her lover, a Mafia hood. Her career survived and even thrived on the notoriety. But parts eventually ran out for an aging glamour queen with few acting resources to fall back on in her old age.

JANE RUSSELL (b. 1921)

"Discovered" by Howard Hughes, Russell survived the furore surrounding her debut in *The Outlaw* to show, in some movies, that she was more than a male fantasy object. Her best films were *Macao* and *Gentlemen Prefer Blondes*. In later life Russell found God, perhaps as a response to the crudeness with which

"I HAVE DECIDED THAT WHILE I AM A STAR, I WILL BE EVERY INCH AND EVERY MOMENT THE STAR. EVERYONE FROM THE STUDIO GATEMAN TO THE HIGHEST EXECUTIVE WILL KNOW IT."
GLORIA SWANSON

Hollywood marketed her shape in movies such as *Double Dynamite, The French Line* and *Underwater!*

AVA GARDNER (1922–90)

Carrying the burden of the tag of the "world's most beautiful woman" could not have been easy, but Gardner appeared to be quite a tough cookie until her later years, when the ravages of alcohol and burning the candle at both ends finally took their toll with her premature death at the age of 67 in 1990. Along the way she survived marriages to Artie Shaw, Mickey Rooney and Frank Sinatra. Gardner was never a great actress, but

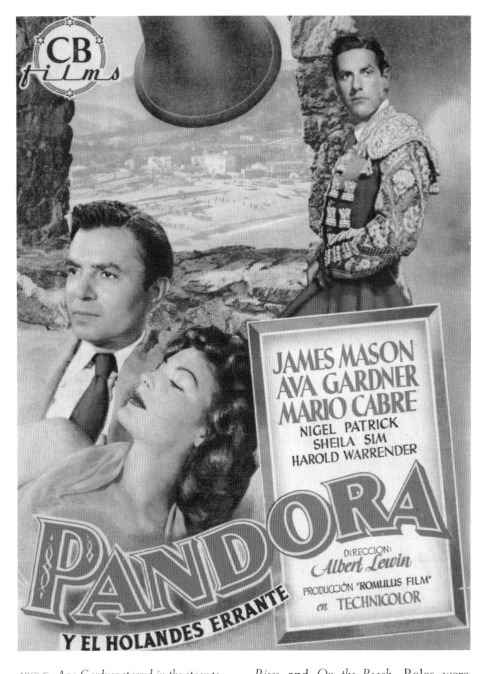

ABOVE *Ava Gardner starred in the strange, portentous melodrama* Pandora and the Flying Dutchman *(1951) with British co-star James Mason.*

she had a certain screen quality of warmth mixed with resilience that went beyond mere beauty. After serving her time in a succession of minor movies, she finally made the big time with the role as Kitty in *The Killers* playing opposite Burt Lancaster. In the 1950s, major film followed major film: *Show Boat, Pandora and the Flying Dutchman, The Snows of Kilimanjaro, Mogambo, The Barefoot Contessa, Bhowani Junction, The Sun Also*

Rises and *On the Beach*. Roles were harder to come by in the 1960s and 70s, but she did continue to work right into the 80s. Gardner was undoubtedly a product of the Hollywood glamour machine and, as such, she was never allowed to show whether she was a more capable actress than her limited roles suggested.

ELIZABETH TAYLOR (b. 1932)

At the height of her career Taylor was the highest-paid star of them all. Born in England of American parents, she joined MGM as a child star and appeared in *Lassie Come Home* and

National Velvet during World War II. Graduating to adult parts, she was dubbed the screen's most beautiful woman and starred in *A Place in the Sun* (1951), *Giant* (1956), *Cat on a Hot Tin Roof* (1958) and *Butterfield 8* (1960). The ponderous epic *Cleopatra* (1963) almost bankrupted 20th Century Fox, partly because of the long delays caused by her ill health. During the shooting of the movie, she began an affair with Richard Burton, whom she subsequently married (twice). Taylor and Burton became the most famous Hollywood show-business couple since Fairbanks and Pickford, earning huge salaries for appearing in some worthless movies (although exceptions included *Who's Afraid of Virginia Woolf?* and *The Taming of the Shrew*), and indulging in conspicuous consumption that merely added to their rather tawdry public image.

BELOW *Grace Kelly was famous as the ice-cool, upper-class blonde. Hitchcock used her in three movies:* Rear Window, Dial M for Murder *and* To Catch a Thief.

After her relationship with Burton finally ended, Taylor's career nose-dived, and recent years have seen her more in the news for her fight against alcoholism, her recovery from a brain tumour and her Aids charity work than for her acting career. But whatever estimation might be made of her abilities, it cannot be denied that she is nothing if not resilient.

SHARON STONE (b. 1958)

Stone shot to notoriety when she appeared in *Basic Instinct* (1992). A former model, she has perhaps suffered from the expectation that all she has to offer is Hollywood glamour. However, she has shown that she can act in movies such as *Casino* (for which she was nominated for an Oscar) and *Last Dance* (in which she played a murderer on Death Row). As she gets older, however, she will find it difficult to get roles because of the totally unfair Hollywood practice of assigning erstwhile glamour ladies to oblivion.

BELOW *Sharon Stone is in the tradition of Hollywood glamour stars, but she has tried to break free from that mould in movies such as* Sliver, *in which she played a victim and* Last Dance, *in which she played a murderer.*

30

ABOVE *A young Elizabeth Taylor poses for the MGM camera. Female stars such as Taylor had thousands of glamorous publicity shots released to the print media.*

THE GOOD JOES

The good joe stars are the "Mr Reliables", the archetypal quietly-spoken heroes who don't make a lot of fuss but who are around to sort everything out when a situation turns nasty.

GARY COOPER (1901–61)

Cooper's screen persona is the straight-down-the-line, on-the-level, slow-talking, slow-burning but

ABOVE *Gary Cooper was a natural choice to play American heroes. In the 1942* Pride of the Yankees *Cooper appeared as baseball star Lou Gehrig opposite Teresa Wright.*

handsome American good guy. *Mr Deeds Goes to Town*, a Frank Capra-directed fable about how a good joe can melt even Washington's hard heart, typified the Cooper role – an incorruptible, unworldly Mr Average who defeats the crooks in the end by sheer integrity. Cooper was also used in westerns and adventures, such as *The Plainsman, Beau Geste, The Westerner* and *Unconquered*. He was a natural choice for the eponymous World War I hero in *Sergeant York* and won an Oscar for his most famous role as the isolated marshal in *High Noon*,

interpreted by many as an anti-McCarthy movie, but if it was, Cooper was unaware of it because he was one of the stars who publicly testified to the Congress investigating committee about alleged Communist infiltration into Hollywood: "From what I hear about Communism, I don't like it because it isn't on the level." But you don't have to be a genius to be a movie star, and there is no doubting Cooper's enduring popularity as a major star. Other notable movies in which he starred include *Meet John Doe, Ball of Fire, Pride of the Yankees, For Whom the Bell Tolls, The Fountainhead* (in which he rather uncharacteristically played a Frank Lloyd Wright-type architect), and *Vera Cruz*. But the enduring memory of "Coop" will be on those empty, lonely streets of the western town in *High Noon*, abandoned by all including Grace Kelly playing his wife. However, to the strains of the song "Do not forsake me, oh my darling" on the Tex Ritter soundtrack, Kelly returns to help her husband shoot down the baddies. They don't make 'em like that any more!

JAMES STEWART (1908–97)

Stewart was another slow-speaking, drawling star who played his share of "honest joe" parts, notably in Frank Capra's *Mr Smith Goes to Washington* and *It's a Wonderful Life*. Hitchcock and Anthony Mann were two other directors who played important roles in Stewart's career. Hitchcock used Stewart in *Rope, Rear Window, The Man Who Knew Too Much* and *Vertigo*, while Mann made eight westerns with Stewart, including *Winchester 73* and *The Man from Laramie*. Both these directors gave Stewart the opportunity to play more complex characters than he usually did. John Ford also used Stewart when he needed an actor who could

ABOVE *Hitchcock cast good joe James Stewart as an obsessive voyeur working out his own repressed desire while solving a murder case in* Rear Window *(1954).*

communicate integrity: *Two Rode Together* and *The Man Who Shot Liberty Valance*. Other major movies for Stewart were *The Philadelphia Story, Harvey, Anatomy of a Murder* and *Shenandoah*. He played real-life American heroes in *The Stratton Story, The Glenn Miller Story* and *The Spirit of St Louis* (about the aviator, Charles A. Lindbergh).

HENRY FONDA (1905–82)

Fonda seemed to be first choice for playing presidents, presidential candidates or senators: *Young Mr Lincoln, Advise and Consent, The Best Man* and *Fail-Safe*. He often played the soft-spoken hero who represents American justice and free speech. In *The Grapes of Wrath, The Ox Bow Incident* and *12 Angry Men* he defended the downtrodden, and through his presence signified that the American Way of Life was basically fair and just. He played American heroes such as Frank James, Alexander Graham Bell and Wyatt Earp. Only rarely did he not play the good guy, notably in *Once Upon a Time in the West*. He was rather irascible in his last movie, *On*

Golden Pond, a role perhaps closer to his real-life persona. He gave up Hollywood between 1948 and 1955 and returned to the stage, until the good guy part in *Mister Roberts* drew

ABOVE *Henry Fonda found his quintessential role in Sidney Lumet's 1957 movie* 12 Angry Men. *Fonda plays a man in a cream suit who alone on a jury holds out against a verdict of guilty against a Hispanic youth.*

ABOVE *Spencer Tracy played a no-nonsense priest in* Boys Town (1938), *co-starring with a young Mickey Rooney. The picture was a glutinous mixture of worthiness and sentimentality.*

him back to the screen. While shooting that film, he reputedly had a fist fight with director John Ford. As the actor himself once said, "I'm not really Henry Fonda. Nobody could have that much integrity."

SPENCER TRACY (1900–67)

Solidity was Tracy's trademark – he could always be relied on and trusted. Tracy had a strong screen presence, although his range was limited and he sometimes allowed himself to edge over into sentimentality – for example, in his roles as a priest in *Boys Town, San Francisco* and *Men of Boys Town*. His limitations as an actor were exposed when he played *Dr Jekyll and Mr Hyde*, but he scored in comedies with Katharine Hepburn: *Woman of the Year, State of the Union, Adam's Rib* and *Pat and Mike*. His power was used profitably in *Fury, Northwest Passage* and *The Last Hurrah*. His liberal politics were reflected in some of the movies he made: *Keeper of the Flame* (about American fascism), *Bad Day at Black Rock* (anti-racism), *Inherit the Wind* (anti-religious fundamentalism), *Judgment at Nuremberg* (as a judge of war crimes) and *Guess Who's Coming to Dinner* (as a father coming to terms with his daughter's marrying Sidney Poitier). Tracy was separated for a

long time from his wife and family and had a long relationship with Katharine Hepburn. But the demon drink proved to be his enemy and contributed to his death in 1967.

GREGORY PECK (1916–2003)

Opinions vary about Peck's acting abilities, and in some parts such as Captain Ahab in *Moby Dick* and Scott Fitzgerald in *Beloved Infidel* he was clearly out of his depth. He was at his best in solid, caring roles: as Atticus, the southern lawyer in *To Kill a Mockingbird*, he won an Oscar, and he had other good-guy roles in *The Keys of the Kingdom, The Yearling, Gentleman's Agreement, The Man in the Grey Flannel Suit, The Big Country* and *On the Beach*. He tried to break the heroic pattern by playing villains in *Duel in the Sun*

LEFT *Gregory Peck starred in the war yarn adapted from an Alistair MacLean book,* The Guns of Navarone. *As a good-guy actor, he is saved from shooting a female traitor by another woman doing the dirty work. Good guys just don't do that kind of thing!*

ABOVE *Charlton Heston had a late success in his career with this sci-fi thriller* The Omega Man. *When civilization is threatened big time, send for Heston! His latter years have been spent as a spokesman for the National Rifle Association in the USA.*

and *The Boys from Brazil*, and also had his share of romantic lead parts, notably in *Spellbound, David and Bathsheba, The Snows of Kilimanjaro, Roman Holiday* and *Arabesque*. Man-of-action roles have included *The Gunfighter, Captain Horatio Hornblower, Twelve O'Clock High, Pork Chop Hill* and *The Guns of Navarone*. Peck became a pillar of the Hollywood establishment, representing the more liberal side of filmland's politics.

CHARLTON HESTON (b. 1924)

Heston is mainly associated with roles in epics, but basically he played good guys whether he was Moses, Ben-Hur or El Cid. However, Heston took himself very seriously as an actor (witness his autobiography *An Actor's Life*). His career really took off when

ABOVE *Sidney Poitier was one of the first of a new generation of black American stars. He rarely strayed from his good-guy screen persona.*

he played Moses in De Mille's *The Ten Commandments* and this was followed by *Ben-Hur*, *El Cid* and *The Agony and the Ecstasy* (as Michelangelo). Other epic parts included *The War Lord*, *Khartoum* (as General Gordon) and *55 Days at Peking*. His westerns have included *The Big Country*, *Major Dundee* and *Will Penny*. Sci-fi roles in *Planet of the Apes*, *Soylent Green* and *The Omega Man* gave his career a boost, but Shakespearian roles in *Julius Caesar* and *Antony and Cleopatra* failed to make the critics enthuse. In his later years he returned to the stage and dabbled in directing, and even appeared in the television series *The Colbys* for a season. His politics moved from the Democratic Left to becoming a spokesman for the National Rifle Association, defending the right of Americans to own guns and shoot people in defence of their property. In *Bowling for Columbine* (2002) Michael Moore made good use of Heston's confused and simple-minded patriotism to attack those attitudes.

KEVIN COSTNER (b. 1955)

Costner is seen as resembling Stewart and Fonda in his quiet but authoritative style. His first big success was as Eliot Ness in *The Untouchables* (1987) and this was followed by his role as the duplicitous spy in *No Way Out*. *Field of Dreams* was a Capraesque exercise in nostalgia and down-home American values, but *Revenge* involved Costner in a macho tale of betrayal and bloodletting.

However, it was *Dances with Wolves* (1990) that put the seal of major stardom on Costner's career. Directing this "liberal" reappraisal of the myth of the American frontier and the white man's interaction with Native Americans brought Costner a Best Director Oscar. *Robin Hood, Prince of Thieves* (1991) was also a major box-office success for him and seemed to indicate that he would be a major star for a long time to come. His career faltered in the 1990s – *Waterworld* was a hugely expensive turkey, as was *The Postman* – but he received critical acclaim for *Open Range* (2003). He clearly likes to portray sportsmen on screen, as *Bull Durham*, *Tin Cup* and *For Love of the Game* indicate. *Thirteen Days* (2000), about the Cuba crisis, was a change of pace for him, in some ways recalling his earlier role in *JFK* (1991).

TOM HANKS (b. 1956)

Hanks is Hollywood's current top "good guy" actor. He can play comedy roles and heavy dramatic parts. The actor he most resembles from old Hollywood is perhaps James Stewart.

His first major success was *Big* (1988) and then he survived *The Bonfire of the Vanities* in which he was woefully miscast. His next big hit was the romantic comedy *Sleepless in Seattle*, which he followed with *Philadelphia*, in which he played a gay man dying of Aids. It is a testimony to changing social attitudes that Hanks could take on this role without harming his career. *Forrest Gump* unaccountably was another major hit for him, as was *Apollo 13* in which he played a good-guy astronaut. He turned writer-director in *That Thing You Do* and then

RIGHT *Tom Hanks is in the mould of James Stewart and Henry Fonda. He had a huge success with the romantic comedy* Sleepless in Seattle *(1993), co-starring Meg Ryan.*

led the cast in Spielberg's *Saving Private Ryan*, an ultimate good-guy role. Other hits for him were the *Toy Story* series, *The Green Mile* and *Cast Away*, but for many critics he was miscast in *Road to Perdition* (2002) and *The Terminal* (2004). Hanks is a talented actor; he deserves credit for some unusual roles but needs to guard against wanting to be liked all the time.

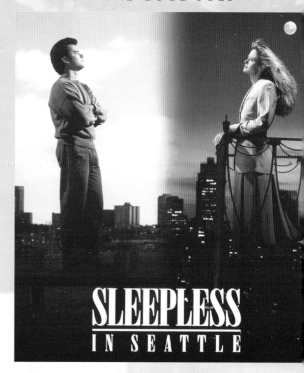

BELOW *Kevin Costner starred in and directed* Dances with Wolves *(1990), which won seven Oscars, including Best Picture, Best Director, Best Adapted Screenplay and Best Cinematography.*

35

THE HEAVIES, VILLAINS AND DOWNRIGHT CADS

Baddies come in all shapes and sizes. Sometimes a heavy is not quite a villain – however, a villain is always a villain, whereas a cad may be a villain but he's charming with it. The actors awarded honoured status in this section represent all three categories.

BELA LUGOSI (1882–1956)

Of Hungarian origin, Lugosi was the screen's most famous Dracula in *Dracula* (1931), *Mark of the Vampire* and *The Return of the Vampire*, and also played the monster in *Frankenstein Meets the Wolf Man*. He was typecast in horror movies such as *Murders in the Rue Morgue*, *White Zombie*, *The Raven* and *The Ghost of Frankenstein*. In the

latter part of his career he appeared in spoof versions of the Frankenstein and Dracula legends: *Abbott and Costello Meet Frankenstein*, *Bela Lugosi Meets a Broadway Gorilla* and *Mother Riley Meets the Vampire*. He was played by Martin Landau in the 1994 movie *Ed Wood*, which documented the last months of Lugosi's life, by which time he was penniless, living in an anonymous LA suburb and hopelessly addicted to hard drugs.

BORIS KARLOFF (1887–1969)

Karloff in real life was an Englishman of the old school, a pillar of the 1930s British colony in Hollywood who liked to show the natives how to dress for dinner and how to play cricket.

ABOVE *Three very heavy heavies: Bela Lugosi, Akim Tamiroff and Basil Rathbone, who starred in the 1956* The Black Sleep. *Lugosi was the screen's most famous Dracula; Tamiroff was terrific in Welles's* Touch of Evil; *and Rathbone was a familiar public-school bad guy in Hollywood movies, crossing many a sword with Errol Flynn.*

On screen he was the monster in the 1931 *Frankenstein* and was involved in *The Old Dark House*, *The Mask of Fu Manchu*, *The Mummy*, *The Bride of Frankenstein* and *The Raven*. In the mid-1940s he made three more notable movies: *The Body Snatcher*, *Isle of the Dead* and *Bedlam*. In the 60s he appeared in three Roger Corman spoofs of the horror genre: *The Raven*,

The Terror and *Comedy of Terrors*. In 1968 he made one of his last films and one of his best, *Targets*, which was Peter Bogdanovich's first movie. Karloff was refreshingly modest about his achievements: "You could heave a brick out of the window and hit 10 actors who could play my parts. I just happened to be on the right corner at the right time."

EDWARD G. ROBINSON (1893–1973)

It is probably doing Robinson a disservice to include him in this section, but it is as a movie baddie that he will largely be remembered. The 1931 *Little Caesar* made him a star, and a succession of gangster roles in the 1930s created Robinson's tough-guy screen persona. He was a memorable insurance claims investigator in *Double Indemnity* and, in the 1940s, was more often the good guy in movies such as *The Woman in the Window*, *Scarlet Street* and *The Stranger*. He returned to

playing villains in *Key Largo*, *Black Tuesday*, *The Ten Commandments* (as Dathan), *Seven Thieves* and *Two Weeks in Another Town*. His small stature and menacing looks meant he would never be cast as a hero, but he brought real quality to many of his roles.

ABOVE *Edward G. Robinson was one of the best actors of his generation. In* All My Sons *(1948), adapted from the Arthur Miller play, he was an aeroplane parts manufacturer with a guilty secret. Robinson was a very cultured man in real life, despite the fact that he played so many criminal thugs on screen.*

GEORGE SANDERS (1906–72)

Sanders was the archetypal British cad – smooth, urbane and as trustworthy as a car salesman in Mayfair. He was the cad in *Rebecca*, but then had a saintly spell in *The Saint* and *The Falcon* series. He was the Gauguin figure in *The Moon and Sixpence*, another rotter in *Summer Storm*, *The Picture of Dorian Gray*, *Hangover Square*, *Forever Amber* and, memorably, in *All About Eve* for which he won the Best Supporting Actor Oscar. However, Sanders was never really committed to his profession and used to disparage his work. Perhaps it was not surprising that he took his own life in 1972, writing in his suicide note that he was bored and that he was glad to be leaving "this sweet cesspool that was the world". A cad to the last.

LEFT *George Sanders on the cover of* Picturegoer *in 1946, looking every inch the cad he played in many movies.*

37

LEFT *Sydney Greenstreet made his film debut in* The Maltese Falcon *(1941). Here he discusses the whereabouts of the black bird with Sam Spade (Humphrey Bogart).*

SYDNEY GREENSTREET (1879–1954)

One of the screen's great fat men, Greenstreet's film debut could hardly have been more auspicious: he played the villainous Kasper Guttman in *The Maltese Falcon* (1941). He came up against Bogart again in *Casablanca* and *Passage to Marseilles* and was another heavy in *The Mask of Dimitrios*. None of his later roles brought him similar success, and when he died aged 75 in 1954, he had packed all of his film career into nine years.

CHARLES LAUGHTON (1899–1962)

Laughton certainly played a variety of roles but he was always at his most watchable when he played an over-the-top villain such as Nero in *The Sign of the Cross* (1932), the incestuous Mr Barrett in *The Barretts of Wimpole Street* (1934), Captain Bligh in *Mutiny on the Bounty* (1935), the unrelenting policeman in *Les Misérables* (1935) and the newspaper proprietor in *The Big Clock* (1948). He also played Quasimodo in *The Hunchback of Notre Dame*, a weak but finally courageous schoolteacher in *This Land is Mine* and a wily Roman senator in *Spartacus*. He is remembered as well for his direction

of *The Night of the Hunter*. Married to Elsa Lanchester for years, he was nonetheless seemingly tortured by his homosexuality. For some, Laughton was the epitome of the ham actor; for others a performer of real genius.

PETER LORRE (1904–64)

A Hungarian by birth, Lorre was a star in German movies before moving to Britain and Hollywood. He starred as the child murderer in Fritz Lang's *M* (1930) and was in Hitchcock's *The Man Who Knew Too Much* (1934) and *The Secret Agent* (1936). After starring in a series of eight *Mr Moto* movies playing the Japanese detective, Lorre had a memorable role in *The Maltese Falcon* and a small but significant part in *Casablanca*. His oddball manner and sinister looks were used to effect in *The Mask of Dimitrios* (1944) and *Arsenic and Old Lace* in the same year. He was inevitably used in horror flicks, and one of the best he made was *The Beast with Five Fingers* (1946). The latter part of his career

was filled with parts that parodied his screen persona; he appeared in two Jerry Lewis movies, *The Sad Sack* (1958) and *The Patsy* (1964). Lorre was undoubtedly a better actor than Hollywood allowed him to be, but no self-respecting impersonator does not have Lorre in his repertoire.

VINCENT PRICE (1911–93)

Price was another over-the-top actor who only achieved real fame late in his career in horror films. He was unpleasant in *Laura* (1944) and *The Three Musketeers* (1948) and then appeared in *House of Wax* (1953). *The Bat* and *The Fall of the House of Usher* further enhanced his Grand Guignol screen persona, and these exercises in camp excess were followed by *The Pit and the Pendulum*, *The Raven*, *The Tomb of Ligeia*, *The Abominable Dr Phibes*, *Theatre of Blood* and *Journey into Fear*, as well as numerous others. He brought a quality of high camp to his roles and his performances teetered on the edge of absurdity.

BELOW *Peter Lorre was a familiar criminal in many movies. Here he is being arrested in* Casablanca *while Rick, played by Humphrey Bogart, doesn't lift a finger to save him.*

A WARNER BROS. PICTURE

CASABLANCA

ROD STEIGER (1925–2002)

"You shoulda looked after me a little, Charlie", complains Brando to Steiger in the famous taxi cab scene in *On the Waterfront*. Steiger's naturalistic acting style, and his tendency to ham, made him one of the best of the 1950s villains in movies such as *Oklahoma!*, *The Harder They Fall* and *Al Capone*. He clearly loved playing Mr Joyboy in *The Loved One* and outacted everyone else in *Doctor Zhivago* as the repellent Komarovsky. He won an Oscar for his bigoted policeman in *In the Heat of the Night* and was a psychopathic killer in *No Way to Treat a Lady*. He played Napoleon in *Waterloo* and Lucky Luciano in the 1973 movie of the same name. His career had its troughs and he certainly made far too many bad movies, but he allowed his talent to shine through in a handful of worthwhile films: *On the Waterfront*, *The Big Knife* (playing a Harry Cohn-type Hollywood producer and eating the scenery in the process), *The Pawnbroker* and *In the Heat of the Night*. A ham or a genius: the jury is divided.

BELOW *After making a career for himself playing smooth, rather camp bad guys, Vincent Price made a second career in horror movies, such as this three-tale epic* Twice Told Tales *(1963).*

LEE MARVIN (1924–87)

Marvin made his reputation playing psychopathic villains and, even when he was nominally the hero, he always managed to bring an ambiguous quality to his roles. He threw hot coffee in Gloria Grahame's face in *The Big Heat* and was Brando's adversary in *The Wild One*. He was one of the villains in *Bad Day at Black Rock* and Liberty Valance in *The Man Who Shot Liberty Valance*. He won an Oscar for his role as the drunken gunfighter in *Cat Ballou*. Around this time he began to play tough guys with some kind of integrity, as in *The Professionals*, *Point Blank*, *The Dirty Dozen*, *Prime Cut* and

LEFT *Rod Steiger could not be accused of not getting his teeth into a part. In* The Big Knife *(1955) he played a Harry Cohn-type mogul being very nasty indeed to Jack Palance and Shelley Winters.*

BELOW *Lee Marvin had become a the bigger star when* Bad Day at Black Rock *was re-released in the late 1950s so, despite his supporting role in the picture, his name was billed above those of the principal actors Spencer Tracy and Robert Ryan.*

Emperor of the North. Off-screen he had a reputation for being a drinker and a wild man; latterly, he seemingly settled down, but perhaps too late to reverse his declining health. He died in 1987 at the age of 62.

THE QUEENS OF MELODRAMA

The principal characteristic of melodrama – and screen melodrama in particular – is excess. These five queens of melodrama were adept at unleashing extremes of emotion on the screen. In Hollywood's heyday the performances of actresses such as Bette Davis and Joan Crawford gave the so-called "women's picture" a good name.

BETTE DAVIS (1908–89)
Bette Davis's talents as an actress are debatable, but as a movie star she was undoubtedly effective. Highly mannered if not affected, Davis had her own style – love her or loathe her. Too often, perhaps, she was playing "Bette Davis" or even a parody of that persona, but in some movie roles she was highly successful. For me Barbara Stanwyck was a much better actress than Davis, but there is no doubt that Davis in her heyday was much the more important star.

ABOVE *One of the characteristics of the melodrama/women's picture was that the leading lady had to be sacrificial. In* The Old Maid *(1939) Davis made the sacrifice and was noble; Miriam Hopkins was dislikeable.*

LEFT *One of Bette Davis's biggest movies was* Now Voyager *(1942). Remember Paul Henreid and his two cigarettes: "We have the stars, let's not reach for the moon." Oh, sacrifice again!*

Davis was mostly very effective in "wicked women" roles such as in *The Little Foxes, The Letter, Mr Skeffington, A Stolen Life* and *Whatever Happened to Baby Jane?* She was noble in *Dark Victory, The Old Maid, The Corn is Green* and *Old Acquaintance*. She suffered for love in *Now Voyager* and *Deception*. Her later Grand Guignol roles included *Hush... Hush, Sweet Charlotte* and *The Nanny*.

At the height of her career in the late 1930s and 40s Davis was one of Hollywood's biggest box-office stars. She took on her studio, Warners, over the seven-year contract system and, although she lost the court case, she ultimately helped to free movie actors from that form of bonded slavery. Always independent and forceful, she acquired a reputation for being difficult, which may have contributed to the fact that her career in the 1950s suddenly went into decline, so much so that she had to put an advertisement in *The Hollywood Reporter* announcing that she needed work. Her most famous role

> "WHEN I SAW MY FIRST FILM TEST, I RAN FROM THE PROJECTION ROOM SCREAMING."
> BETTE DAVIS

may be Margo Channing in *All About Eve*, a movie in which she utters the immortal line, "Fasten your seatbelts, it's going to be a bumpy night." Most impersonators of stars can do a passable Bette Davis: that throaty New England voice with its cutting edge, those large eyes and the exaggerated inhaling of a cigarette. Her style was the opposite of naturalistic acting – with Davis, there was always a performance going on.

JOAN CRAWFORD (1904–77)
Another great "sufferer" was Crawford, but only in the latter part of her long film career. Christened Lucille Le Sueur, Crawford was cast as a "flapper" in her early film parts, and some misguided studio executives thought she could dance. In the 1930s and early 40s she made eight mostly forgettable films with Clark Gable. Her archetypal roles were as the ambitious stenographer in *Grand Hotel* and as Sadie Thompson in *Rain*. Whereas Davis was mostly playing society ladies, Crawford played shop girls and typists. When MGM dropped her in the 1940s she signed a new contract with Warners and came into her own as Davis's chief rival in the melodrama stakes. Movies such as *Mildred Pierce, Humoresque, Possessed, Daisy Kenyon, Sudden Fear, Torch Song* and *Autumn Leaves* had her suffering at the hands of her husbands, lovers, children and society in general. Her screen persona lent itself more to "victim" roles than Davis's, but

ABOVE *Joan Crawford worked very hard at being Joan Crawford. Here she adorns the cover of a 1941 issue of* Picturegoer.

Crawford, with a limited range of acting ability, still managed to project a powerful screen image.

Off-screen, Crawford built up a reputation for her ruthless pursuit of success and cleanliness. As her screen career wilted, she married a PepsiCola executive and the soft drink manufacturer had to defend itself from the attentions of the widow when her executive husband died. Her adopted daughter wrote a damning account of her as a mother in *Mommie Dearest*, which was later filmed with Faye Dunaway as Crawford. Crawford and Davis co-starred in *Whatever Happened to Baby Jane?*, in one scene of which Davis pushes Crawford, crippled in a wheelchair, down a staircase. It was a case of Hollywood feeding off its own legends again. Crawford symbolized that desperate hunger for Hollywood success that characterizes many stars.

"THE PUBLIC LIKES PROVOCATIVE FEMININE PERSONALITIES BUT IT ALSO LIKES TO KNOW THAT, UNDERNEATH IT ALL, THE ACTRESSES ARE LADIES."
JOAN CRAWFORD

INGRID BERGMAN (1915–82)

A Swedish actress, Bergman made her first Hollywood film *Intermezzo* with Leslie Howard in 1939, and became Hollywood's top female star in the 1940s. *Casablanca* opposite Bogart cast her again as a woman destined to end up suffering for love, as did *For Whom the Bell Tolls*, *Spellbound* and *Notorious*, the latter two directed by Alfred Hitchcock. She also suffered in *Dr Jekyll and Mr Hyde*, *Gaslight*, *Joan of Arc* and *Under Capricorn*. Then she had a real-life affair with Italian director Roberto Rossellini, who was married at the time, as was Bergman. She had Rossellini's child (Roberto Guisto Giuseppe) and scandalized hypocritical Hollywood. She made a series of films with Rossellini (*Stromboli, Europa '51, We the Women*) before returning to a contrite Hollywood who rewarded her with an Oscar for her role in *Anastasia*. She had further successes with *Indiscreet* and *The Inn of the Sixth Happiness* but her great days at the box office were over. Late in her career she made *Autumn Sonata* (1978), directed by

BELOW *Ingrid Bergman featured on another* Picturegoer *cover from 1941. Bergman broke the mould of Hollywood beauties with a more natural and less manufactured look.*

ABOVE *Gene Tierney (1920–91) communicated a kind of edgy, neurotic quality on the screen and she suffered from psychological problems off-screen as well. Some of her best films include* Laura *(1944),* Dragonwyck *(1946),* The Razor's Edge *(1946) and* Whirlpool *(1949).*

Ingmar Bergman, and she revealed what she might have achieved if her Hollywood roles had been more consistently worthwhile. Bergman had a beauty that escaped Hollywood stereotyping and a quality of "goodness" that illuminated her roles.

BARBARA STANWYCK (1907–90)

Stanwyck was more working class in origin and manner than Davis or Crawford. She also employed an iciness in her screen portrayals that the other two could not match. Her greatest role was in *Double Indemnity* as Phyllis Dietrichson, the femme fatale who snares insurance salesman Walter Neff, played by normally "good guy" actor, Fred MacMurray, in

her murderous plans. Stanwyck and MacMurray deserve to be as famous for those roles as Bogart and Bergman are for *Casablanca*.

Other archetypal Stanwyck roles were in *Stella Dallas* (as a sacrificial mother), *The Lady Eve, Ball of Fire, The Strange Love of Martha Ivers, The Two Mrs Carrolls* and *Sorry, Wrong Number*. She lost Fred MacMurray to Joan Bennett in Douglas Sirk's *There's Always Tomorrow* and must have known her screen career was on the wane when she starred with Elvis Presley in *Roustabout*. However, her television series *The Big Valley* was a success in the 1960s and she later co-starred with Richard Chamberlain in *The Thorn Birds*. A very underrated actress, Stanwyck had tremendous power on screen and this despite her quite ordinary looks. She was married to Robert Taylor, considered by some to be a glamour boy, for a number of years. She was known as a Hollywood professional who never threw a tantrum and just got on with her job.

BELOW *Barbara Stanwyck was in many people's opinions the best actress of her generation. Here she is in the 1937 version of the creaky melodrama* Stella Dallas. *She had a tremendous talent for suddenly upping the emotional stakes and reaching a state of hysterical emotion in a matter of seconds.*

FAYE DUNAWAY (b. 1941)

Dunaway is a contemporary star with something of the Davis–Crawford "over-the-top" style. Indeed, she played Joan Crawford in an unintentionally hilarious "biopic" of the old time star, *Mommie Dearest* (1981). She came to stardom in *Bonnie and Clyde* and followed this up by playing opposite Steve McQueen in the ultra-smooth *The Thomas Crown Affair*. After that, her career seemed to mark time until she made *Chinatown*, *Three Days of the Condor*, *Network* and *Mommie Dearest*. Dunaway has always played the star off-screen as well, which is in itself a throwback to the old days of Hollywood. She has found it hard to sustain her box-office appeal, however, and satisfactory roles have been few and far between in the 1990s and early 2000s, but she resurfaced briefly in the weak remake of *The Thomas Crown Affair* (1999) and in a small part in *The Rules of Attraction* (2002).

ABOVE *Ronald Reagan's first wife, Jane Wyman (b. 1914) won an Oscar for playing a deaf mute in* Johnny Belinda *(1948), then Douglas Sirk used her in two of his best melodramas,* Magnificent Obsession *(1954) and* All That Heaven Allows *(1955).*

BELOW *Faye Dunaway can be likened to the old Hollywood melodrama queens if only for her tendency to go over the top. Here she shoots it out alongside Warren Beatty in* Bonnie and Clyde. *As an older actress in Hollywood, she has found roles hard to come by.*

THE GREAT MUSICAL STARS

FRED ASTAIRE (1899–1987)

Nominated by most people as the greatest dancer in movies, Astaire danced with Ginger Rogers in a series of highly successful musicals in the 1930s: *The Gay Divorcee, Roberta, Top Hat, Follow the Fleet, Swing Time, Shall We Dance?, A Damsel in Distress, Carefree* and *The Story of Vernon and Irene Castle.* Astaire was the effortless top-hat-and-tails dancer who made love to his leading ladies through his dancing, but he had a curiously sexless quality. Some fans prefer the movies he made in the latter part of his career: *Easter Parade, The Band Wagon, Daddy Long Legs, Funny Face* and *Silk Stockings.* Astaire was a perfectionist and a great worrier about his dance routines, which he usually worked out for himself with the help of choreographer Hermes Pan. His singing voice was also very pleasant and he could interpret a standard by Gershwin or Berlin like few others. A modest man, he could never really understand why people made such a fuss over his movies. "I just dance," he once said. Most people are glad he did. After his first screen test, some conventional studio functionary reported, "Can't act. Can't sing. Slightly bald. Can dance a little."

BETTY GRABLE (1916–73)

Grable was living proof of Hollywood's power to fragment the female body and make big bucks out of it: her legs were supposedly insured for millions of dollars with Lloyd's of London. A musical star of only average singing and dancing abilities, she was tailored to be the wartime pin-up of the American forces. Basically, she was a glamorized version of the American girl-next-door. Overt sexuality was absent in her movies; she was sold on the basis of peaches-and-cream, kid-sister appeal. This star persona proved very successful at the box office in a series of anodyne musicals such as *Million Dollar Legs, Down Argentine Way, Tin Pan Alley, Moon over Miami, Footlight Serenade,*

LEFT *Fred Astaire and Ginger Rogers are the most famous dancing couple in movie history.* The Barkleys of Broadway *(1949) was the last movie they made together.*

Springtime in the Rockies, Coney Island, Sweet Rosie O'Grady and *Pin-Up Girl.* Her career lasted well into the 1950s with musicals such as *Mother Wore Tights, The Beautiful Blonde from Bashful Bend, My Blue Heaven* and the nonmusical *How to Marry a Millionaire.* When these movies are seen today, you ask yourself what all the fuss was about, but then, 40 years from now, they'll be asking the same question about Madonna. The answer will be the same: publicity and money.

BELOW *Jeanette MacDonald and Nelson Eddy were a very popular singing team in the 1930s and 40s: here they are seen in* Bitter Sweet *(1940).*

ABOVE *Betty Grable became the GI pin-up during World War II. Here she is seen with Reginald Gardiner in Lubitsch's* That Lady in Ermine *(1948).*

45

GENE KELLY (1912–96)

Kelly was dogged all his movie career by comparisons with Astaire. The fact is that he was very different: Kelly was overtly masculine, athletic and sensual, whereas Astaire was graceful and largely sexless. However, it could be claimed for Kelly that he has been the single most important influence on the movie musical as a star, choreographer and director.

Kelly became a star on Broadway playing Pal Joey, then he went to MGM and made *For Me and My Gal* with Judy Garland. *Cover Girl*, with his choreography for his alter-ego dance, marked a breakthrough for Kelly and he went on to star in and co-direct with Stanley Donen *On the Town*, *Singin' in the Rain* and *It's Always Fair Weather*. In between he was directed by Vincente Minnelli in *The Pirate*, *An American in Paris* and *Brigadoon*. The "Singin' in the Rain" number in the movie of that name has become one of the most famous sequences of all time. Kelly's Irish-American charm and his grin that "could melt stone" endeared him to audiences, until the musical bubble burst and he was set free by

ABOVE *Gene Kelly chose Leslie Caron to play opposite him in* An American in Paris *(1951). This Vincente Minnelli-directed movie won the Best Film Oscar, and the same year Gene Kelly won a Special Oscar for his contribution to screen musicals. Especially in his role as choreographer, Kelly remains the single most important influence on the American film musical.*

MGM. His career went into reverse until he was given the chance to direct *Hello Dolly!* in 1969. In his latter years, he appeared in three *That's Entertainment* movies that were compilations of the best numbers from the great MGM musicals.

JUDY GARLAND (1922–69)

Garland is another icon of the movie musical. A child prodigy, she was overworked by her studio, MGM, in a series of musicals with Mickey Rooney. She was also Dorothy in *The Wizard of Oz*. Graduating from teen musicals, she made *Meet Me in St Louis* in which she was directed by Vincente Minnelli, who shortly afterwards married her. Their marriage produced Liza Minnelli. Garland starred with

Gene Kelly in three movies: *For Me and My Gal*, *The Pirate* and *Summer Stock*. She made *Easter Parade* with Astaire, by which time she was in serious trouble with the studio and herself. Addicted to pills of various kinds, she blamed MGM for exploiting her and not using her talent intelligently, but when she failed to turn up for the shooting of *Annie Get Your Gun*, MGM sacked her. Her comeback film was the classic *A Star is Born*, in which she co-starred with James Mason. Her film appearances after that were few and far between. She resumed her concert career, but stories of her drinking and broken marriages dogged her, and she finally died in 1969. Around Garland arose a legend of the kind that only show business could create, and her fans are among the most loyal of all, even 30-odd years after her death.

OPPOSITE *Doris Day made a series of highly popular musicals in the 1940s and 50s, including* April in Paris *(1952),* Calamity Jane *(1953),* Young at Heart *(1955) and* The Pajama Game *(1957). Then she became a star in gender-war comedies.*

48

BING CROSBY (1903–77)

The "Old Groaner" got by on a voice that was pleasant and a personality that smacked of good humour and easy-going ways. Off-screen he was a tyrannical father and mean with a buck. He always knew that he was a very lucky man, and he was certainly fortunate to team up with Bob Hope in the series of *Road* movies they made. He also co-starred with Astaire in *Holiday Inn* and *Blue Skies*. Crosby used that Irish charm of his in two schmaltzy movies about priests, *Going My Way* and *The Bells of St Mary's*. He also tried his hand at straight acting in *The Country Girl* and the remake of *Stagecoach*, in which he played the drunken doctor part. One of his best musicals was *High Society* with Sinatra.

ABOVE *Bing Crosby and Frank Sinatra starred together in* High Society, *the hugely enjoyable musical remake of the equally popular* The Philadelphia Story, *which starred Gary Grant in the Crosby role.*

FRANK SINATRA (1915–98)

Sinatra's movies range from musicals to westerns to straight dramas. Indeed, he won an Oscar for Best Supporting Actor in *From Here to Eternity*. But "The Voice" naturally started out in musicals, all of which were entirely forgettable until *Anchors Aweigh*, *Take Me Out to the Ball Game* and *On the Town* gave him some kind of screen respectability. However, a series of terrible films made him box-office poison for a while until he begged to play Maggio in *From Here to Eternity*. From then on, he could choose his roles. Among the musicals were *Young at Heart*, *Guys and Dolls* and *High Society*. Sinatra became the most famous entertainer in the world, partly because of his dubious off-screen Mafia acquaintances, but too many of his movies were utterly worthless, particularly the "home movies" he made with his gang, the Rat Pack, in the 1960s: *Ocean's Eleven*, *Sergeants Three*, *Four For Texas* and *Robin and the Seven Hoods*.

When he took the trouble and deigned to do more than one complacent take of a scene, he could turn in creditable performances: for example, in *From Here to Eternity*, *The Man with the Golden Arm* and *The Manchurian Candidate*.

BARBRA STREISAND (b. 1942)

Streisand had a great success as Fanny Brice in *Funny Girl* after having made her name in the stage version on Broadway and in London. She then had two flops in a row with *Hello Dolly!* (in which she was miscast) and *On a Clear Day You Can See Forever*, which, despite Vincente Minnelli's direction and having Yves Montand as her co-star, failed to find a large enough audience. However, her screen career recovered with *What's Up, Doc?* in which she revealed her innate comic talent, and *The Way We Were* playing a radical who fought for Roosevelt's New Deal and against McCarthyite tactics in Hollywood during the 1950s. She made the sequel to *Funny Girl*, *Funny Lady*, in 1975 and yet another remake of *A Star is Born* in 1976. This was a huge box-office success, but by this time she wanted to control her career and managed to co-write, co-produce and direct *Yentl* in 1983. She also later directed and

ABOVE *Barbra Streisand made her name in the stage version of* Funny Girl *before starring in the 1968 movie version.*

starred in *The Prince of Tides* and *The Mirror Has Two Faces*. She has a reputation for egomania, but it is difficult to know how accurate this charge is or how much it is the reaction of chauvinists to a powerful woman making her way in the male-dominated movie industry. Now she appears to have disappeared from the big screen and has made her last world tour as a singer. However, she frequently makes appearances in Washington when the Democrats are in power, and she retains a vast army of devoted and even hysterical fans, who will always see her as a diva of the pop world. Mostly, people either love her or loathe her, but perhaps the adulation she has received from her millions of fans has had a negative effect on some of her choices of material and her performances. First and foremost, Streisand is a singer.

ABOVE *Streisand starred in the 1969 film version of the stage musical* Hello, Dolly! *Gene Kelly directed and Walter Matthau co-starred in the movie.*

THE NEW WOMEN

KATHARINE HEPBURN (1907–2003)
Katharine Hepburn largely played emancipated, strong-minded women, albeit often with a quavering voice and trembling lip. Early Hollywood successes with *Morning Glory* and *Little Women* (both 1933) were followed by less commercially successful movies such as *Alice Adams*, *Sylvia Scarlett* and *Mary of Scotland*. She emanated an almost androgynous quality in some of these movies. Labelled "box-office poison" by distributors, she hit back in comedies such as *Bringing Up Baby* and *The Philadelphia Story*. In these classic pictures she was shown at her best: intelligent, witty, possessing a great sense of comic timing and with an individual charm of her own. *Woman of the Year* paired her with Spencer Tracy, with whom she had a long relationship and made several notable movies, including *Keeper of the Flame*, *Adam's Rib*, *Pat and Mike* and *Guess Who's Coming to Dinner*. The gruff and alcoholic Tracy may not have

ABOVE *Katharine Hepburn and James Stewart starred in* The Philadelphia Story *(1940), which was later remade as a musical* High Society *(1956). Grace Kelly took over the Hepburn role in the latter.*

appeared to be the perfect mate for Hepburn, but their relationship somehow worked off-screen as well as on-screen. She played spinsters in *The African Queen* (directed by John Huston), *Summer Madness* (directed by David Lean) and *The Rainmaker*. Never an actress who could be accused of underplaying, opinions divide over her performances in movies such as *Suddenly Last Summer*, *The Lion in Winter* and *The Madwoman of Chaillot*. By this time she was into her quivering upper lip stage. However, she starred with Ralph Richardson in *Long Day's Journey into Night* (1962), directed by Sidney Lumet, and with John Wayne in *Rooster Cogburn* (1975). Her last major role was opposite Henry and Jane Fonda in *On Golden Pond* (1981).

LEFT *John Huston directed Hepburn and Bogart in* The African Queen. *Clint Eastwood's 1990 movie* White Hunter, Black Heart *dealt with events that happened during the shooting of that film.*

LEFT *Jane Fonda in her unreconstructed pre-feminist phase as Barbarella (1968), an adaptation of Jean-Claude Forest's comic strip. Soon after, Fonda left these glamour-girl roles behind her and went on to become the conscience of the nation in movies such as* A Doll's House (1973), Julia (1977) *and* The China Syndrome (1979).

were reconciled. She had a popular success in *Nine to Five* but has also played in some flops – *Rollover* and *Agnes of God*, for example. She co-starred with Jeff Bridges in *The Morning After* and with De Niro in *Stanley and Iris*. Her liberal politics made her hated by many Americans during the Vietnam War, but she has been better known in latter years for the exploitation of her own image in promoting her health and beauty business. Married and divorced from media mogul Ted Turner, Fonda has recently announced her conversion to a born-again type of Christianity.

BELOW *Jane Fonda with her then-husband in the late 1960s, French director Roger Vadim.*

Her upper-class New England manner was best suited to her early roles in which she symbolized a new kind of female star who depended hardly at all on physical allure.

JANE FONDA (b. 1937)

Fonda has had to work hard to be taken seriously in serious roles, partly because of her glamorous appearance and partly because her early film career landed her with decidedly unliberated parts such as those in *Cat Ballou* and *Barbarella* (with her then-husband Roger Vadim directing). Her first real success was in *Klute* for which she won an Oscar and this was followed by more overtly feminist roles in *A Doll's House*, *Julia* and *The China Syndrome*. In 1981 she appeared with her father, Henry, in *On Golden Pond*, playing a daughter having difficulties with her father, which apparently she had always had in real life with Henry until they

MERYL STREEP (b. 1949)

Streep's quest for variety in her roles has led to her being identified with parts demanding that she perfects yet another accent of one kind or another. She was British in *The French Lieutenant's Woman* and *Plenty*, Polish in *Sophie's Choice*, Danish in *Out of Africa* and Australian in *A Cry in the Dark*.

Streep first came to prominence as De Niro's lover in *The Deer Hunter* and they appeared together again in *Falling in Love*. She played unsympathetic women in *Manhattan* and *Kramer vs. Kramer*, whilst in *Silkwood* she played the tough, working-class rebel Karen Silkwood who was bumped off for exposing secrets of the American nuclear industry. She has had her bad reviews, notably for *Ironweed* and *She-Devil*. She was miscast in *Postcards from the Edge*, and made some turkeys such as *House of the Spirits*, before she starred with Clint Eastwood in *The Bridges of Madison County*. After that came *Before and After*, *Marvin's Room*, *One True Thing*,

ABOVE *Meryl Streep played a wronged wife to Jack Nicholson's husband in the 1986 comedy* Heartburn.

Dancing at Lughnasa and *Music of the Heart*. Streep prepares meticulously for her roles, and she may have an element of clinical overkill that prevents her from achieving real presence on screen.

JESSICA LANGE (b. 1949)

Lange's acting talents were hardly used in the 1976 remake of *King Kong*, for which she was taken from near obscurity to play the female lead. The film was not a success, but she fared better in *All That Jazz*, *The Postman Always Rings Twice* and *Frances* (playing 1930s star Frances Farmer). Lange

ABOVE *Jessica Lange and Jack Nicholson play the murdering lovers in Bob Rafelson's version of* The Postman Always Rings Twice *(1981)*.

chooses her roles with care and makes movies that "say something". Even *Tootsie*, the comedy in which she starred opposite Dustin Hoffman, reflected something about men-women relationships, whilst *Country*, *Sweet Dreams*, *Crimes of the Heart* and *The Music Box* all attempt to reflect aspects of contemporary society. Her sincere approach has clearly worked, winning her the Best Actress Oscar in 1994 for *Blue Sky*. She has also made some poor movies, including *Rob Roy*. She returns to the stage from time to time, taking on major roles in Tennessee Williams and Eugene O'Neill plays. She is an intelligent, creative actor.

SIGOURNEY WEAVER (b. 1949)

Weaver achieved star status in her role as Ripley in *Alien* and again played the feminist hero in the sequel, *Aliens*. She starred opposite Mel Gibson in *The Year of Living Dangerously* and had a great success in *Ghostbusters*. She played the baddie in *Working Girl* and the goodie in *Gorillas in the Mist*. She made two more Alien movies, was in the dud *1492*, and was very effective as the icy wife in *The Ice Storm*. However, good roles have been drying up for Weaver, which is a pity because she shows an intelligence and strength on screen – a major star.

ABOVE *Sigourney Weaver appeared as Lieutenant Ripley in all of the* Alien *movies, including* Alien Resurrection *(1997).*

KATHLEEN TURNER (b. 1954)

Turner combines a "new woman" persona with the allure of the old-time Hollywood beauty queens. She made her first big impression in *Body Heat* playing a spider woman who frames William Hurt, in a virtual remake of *Double Indemnity*. Then she went against image and starred as the overweight romantic novelist in *Romancing the Stone*. In *Prizzi's Honor* she played a rather unconvincing hit-woman, whilst in the Ken Russell-directed *Crimes of Passion*, she was a career woman turned prostitute. She reluctantly made *Jewel of the Nile*, the sequel to *Romancing*, and then appeared in the title role in *Peggy Sue Got Married*. She actually lost screen husband William Hurt in *The Accidental Tourist* to Geena Davis, which seemed almost unbelievable, and managed to more or less destroy her fictional husband in *The War of the Roses*. Another strong part came along when she played the title role as private detective in *V.I. Warshawski*. She had some success with *Serial Mom*, but she has had health problems, and screen appearances have been few throughout the 1990s and 2000s. She has, however, returned to the stage, notably playing the Anne Bancroft part, Mrs Robinson, in the stage version of *The Graduate*.

53

She taught him everything she knew – about passion and murder.

BODY HEAT X

LEFT *Kathleen Turner made a big impact in* Body Heat *(1981) playing opposite William Hurt in a contemporary* noir *thriller directed by a young Lawrence Kasdan.*

LEFT *Debra Winger co-starred with Theresa Russell in the 1987* Black Widow.

DEBRA WINGER (b. 1955)

A spiky, off-the-wall image has been created for Winger in movies such as *An Officer and a Gentleman* and *Terms of Endearment*. She is usually allowed to be unglamorous in her roles, although the dowdy young woman at some point in the screenplay usually turns into the beautiful princess, as in *Officer* and *Black Widow*. Playing Shirley MacLaine's daughter in *Terms of Endearment* did not seem to harm her career, although the bombing at the box office of *Legal Eagles* in which she co-starred with Robert Redford, dented her record of being associated with hit films. She was effective in *The Sheltering Sky* and *Shadowlands*, for which she was nominated for an Oscar.

SUSAN SARANDON (b. 1946)

Two films in the late 1970s for the French director, Louis Malle – *Pretty Baby* and *Atlantic City* – helped to establish Sarandon as a sensitive and powerful actress. She did not have a major success after that until *The Witches of Eastwick*, which she followed up with portrayals of sadder but wiser "older women" in *White Palace* and *Thelma and Louise*. Her usual persona is the tough, worldly-wise, attractive working woman. Her 1996 Oscar for her portrayal of a nun in *Dead Man Walking* confirmed her status as one of the most effective current female stars. Off-screen, she is one of Hollywood's most active political activists, supporting liberal and anti-war causes, thereby attracting conservative opposition.

BELOW *Susan Sarandon, Michelle Pfeiffer and Cher played three witches in the 1987* The Witches of Eastwick.

JODIE FOSTER (b. 1962)

Foster came to prominence as a "child star" in two Martin Scorsese movies, *Alice Doesn't Live Here Anymore* and *Taxi Driver*. After a Disney film, *Freaky Friday*, and a teen angst pic, *Foxes*, she made her mark again in *The Hotel New Hampshire* before she won an Oscar for her role in *The Accused*, in which she played a rape victim. It was *The Silence of the Lambs* in which she gained the status of major star (and the 1992 Best Actress Oscar); she played Clarice Starling, an FBI agent who tracks down a serial killer with the help of Hannibal Lecter. She made a noted transition into an actor/director role, directing *Little Man Tate* and *Home for the Holidays*. As an actress, she had successes with *Sommersby*, *Maverick*, *Contact* and *Panic Room*.

DIANE KEATON (b. 1946)

A rather more "whiny" and "kookie" version of Hollywood's new women, Keaton was associated with Woody Allen in the earlier part of her screen career. She played the title role in *Annie Hall*, for example, and also appeared in *Love and Death*, *Interiors* and

ABOVE *Jodie Foster played an FBI agent in* The Silence of the Lambs.

Manhattan. She took on "tougher" roles in movies that were not directed by Allen: the *Godfather* movies, in which she played the wife of Michael Corleone, *Looking for Mr Goodbar*, *Reds*, *Shoot the Moon*, *The Little Drummer Girl* and *Crimes of the Heart*. She starred with Allen again in *Manhattan Murder Mystery* and also made *The First Wives' Club* and *Marvin's Room*.

LEFT *Diane Keaton played Louise Bryant, the radical journalist in* Reds *(1981), which also featured Jack Nicholson in a cameo role as playwright Eugene O'Neill. The movie was directed by and co-starred Warren Beatty.*

"IF YOU REALLY DON'T LIKE PUBLICITY YOU DON'T DECIDE TO BECOME AN ACTRESS. IT GOES WITH THE TERRITORY."
DIANE KEATON

POST-FEMINIST HEROINES

A new kind of post-feminist leading lady emerged in Hollywood in the 1990s. These stars are not on the barricades for female liberation, but are generally cast in roles that represent them as powerful and independent while also seeming to want what Hollywood has always said women want: a long-term relationship with a man, family, security.....plus ça change....

KIM BASINGER (b. 1953)
Basinger is often likened to oldtime Hollywood stars such as Rita Hayworth or Veronica Lake, but she is certainly a better actress than either of those. After being the bad girl in *The Natural* (1984) and appearing in the soft-porn *9½ Weeks* with Mickey Rourke, she was in *No Mercy* and *Batman*. *Final Analysis* cast her as a neurotic vamp again, but it was with *L.A. Confidential* (1997) that she finally won respect as an actress – and an Oscar. Having been seen as a glamour girl who can act some, whether she will win further powerful roles as she approaches 50 remains to be seen. (Meryl Streep seems to have cornered this market.)

MICHELLE PFEIFFER (b. 1957)
Pfeiffer first made an impact in *Scarface* (1983) with Al Pacino; she proved herself much more than just a pretty face. She had meaty roles in *The Witches of Eastwick* and *Married to the Mob*, then followed those with *Dangerous Liaisons*, *The Fabulous Baker Boys* (for which she was nominated for an Oscar), *The Russia House* (playing a Russian woman), *Frankie and Johnny* and *Batman Returns* as Catwoman. She has worked with some top directors such as Scorsese on *The Age of Innocence* and Mike Nichols on *Wolf*. She has also made some stinkers such as *Dangerous Minds* and some mediocre movies that have made little impact: *What Lies Beneath*, for example. A spirited woman, Pfeiffer has often complained about the roles Hollywood actresses are usually offered.

ANNETTE BENING (b. 1958)
Bening made some impact in *Valmont* (1989), but it was with *The Grifters* (1990) that she broke through to stardom. She acted opposite De Niro in the movie about McCarthyite persecution in 1950s Hollywood, *Guilty By Suspicion*. After starring with Harrison Ford in *Regarding Henry*, she worked with her future husband

ABOVE *Michelle Pfeiffer showed she could carry a tune as well as act in* The Fabulous Baker Boys, *seen here with co-star Jeff Bridges.*

Warren Beatty in *Bugsy*. She was in *The President* with Michael Douglas, *Mars Attacks!* with Jack Nicholson and *The Siege* with Denzel Washington. She was nominated for an Oscar for her comic role in *American Beauty*. Her star status is well established and she should continue to win good roles because she is one of the more intelligent of Hollywood actors.

ABOVE *Kim Basinger co-starred with Richard Gere in* Final Analysis, *a psychological thriller in the film noir tradition.*

ABOVE *Annette Bening made a big impression as a petty criminal in* The Grifters, *starring with Anjelica Huston and John Cusack.*

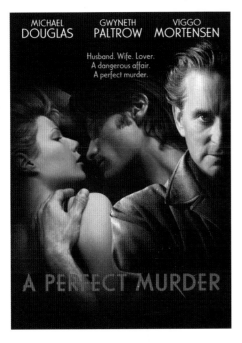

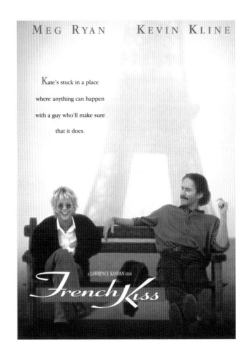

LEFT *In* A Perfect Murder *(1998), a remake of Hitchcock's* Dial M for Murder, *Gwyneth Paltrow played the Grace Kelly role, Michael Douglas took on the Ray Milland role and Viggo Mortensen played the Bob Cummings part.*

then she won a Best Actress Oscar for *Shakespeare in Love.* She took something of a back seat to the two male leads in *The Talented Mr Ripley*, but had a decent role in *Possession* (2002). Paltrow is rather wan for some tastes, but has an appeal that should last.

MEG RYAN (b. 1961)

Ryan survived some turkeys in her early years in Hollywood (*Rich and Famous, Amityville-3D*), but then hit the big time with *When Harry Met Sally...* (1989) starring with Billy Crystal. Her young-woman-next-door star persona was further exploited in another romantic comedy – *Sleepless in Seattle* with Tom Hanks. Hollywood decided that romantic comedies were her thing so she was cast in *When a Man Loves a Woman* and *French Kiss*, which flopped. *Courage Under Fire* (1996) and *In the Cut* (2003) marked a change of pace for her, but *Addicted to Love* and *You've Got Mail* were attempts to resurrect the Ryan of *Sally* and *Seattle.*

ABOVE *Meg Ryan starred with Kevin Kline in the Lawrence Kasdan romantic comedy* French Kiss. *Kline played a somewhat unconvincing screen Frenchman.*

HALLE BERRY (b. 1968)

A former beauty queen, Berry was in Spike Lee's *Jungle Fever* (1991), in *Bulworth* (1998) with Warren Beatty, and played Dorothy Dandridge in a television movie. She became the first black actress to win the Best Actress Oscar for her role in *Monster's Ball* (2001). She also starred in the James Bond movie *Die Another Day* (2002).

GWYNETH PALTROW (b. 1973)

After appearing in two superior Hollywood movies, *Mrs Parker and the Vicious Circle* (1994) and *Jefferson in Paris* (1995), this daughter of actress Blythe Danner and director Bruce Paltrow played the title role in *Emma* and was henceforth able to demand star status. The romantic comedy *Sliding Doors* reinforced the Paltrow persona: a rather bemused modern young woman searching for lasting love. She found rather less than that in *A Perfect Murder*, a remake of Hitchcock's *Dial M for Murder*, and

PENELOPE CRUZ (b. 1974)

Spanish-born Cruz starred in two Spanish movies *Jamon, Jamon* (1992) and Almodóvar's *All About My Mother* (1999) which brought her to the attention of Hollywood. There she quickly made *The Hi-Lo Country, All the Pretty Horses, Blow, Woman on Top, Captain Corelli's Mandolin* and *Vanilla Sky.* She seems to have established herself in Hollywood and is much in demand.

LEFT *Before she won her Oscar for* Monster's Ball *(2001), Halle Berry had to serve her time by playing second fiddle to tough guys Kurt Russell and Steven Seagal in* Executive Decision *(1996).*

THE STREETWISE STARS

There is a group of stars whose screen persona is hard to categorize because of the range of parts they take on. The following male stars emerged from the 1960s onwards, and all have varying degrees of "street wisdom". They represent characteristics of the time, and their roles usually involve them in moral dilemmas of a specifically contemporary nature.

WARREN BEATTY (b. 1937)

Beatty first came to prominence playing an angst-ridden teenager in Elia Kazan's *Splendor in the Grass* (1961). His "pretty boy" image was enhanced when he played a gigolo to middle-aged Vivien Leigh in *The Roman Spring of Mrs Stone*. His first huge success was as Clyde Barrow in *Bonnie and Clyde* in 1967, which he also co-produced. Beatty's looks and off-screen reputation for womanizing meant he had to fight to get roles that stretched him as an actor. *The Parallax View* and *Shampoo*, which he also co-wrote, both attempted to comment on contemporary American society, but it was *Reds* in 1981, which he starred in, produced, co-wrote and directed, that finally freed him from the charge of being "lightweight". In *Reds* he played a left-wing American journalist, John Reed, who was also a Communist. Hollywood, anticipating a thaw in the relations between the superpowers, gave Beatty an Oscar for his direction. Beatty had to survive the 40-million-dollar flop that was *Ishtar* (1987), but *Dick Tracy* (1990) and *Bugsy* (1991) brought him some popular success. From time to time Beatty has been active in American politics on the left of the Democrat Party and it has even been whispered that he might run for high office at some point. *Bulworth* (1998), which he starred in, co-wrote and directed, was a satirical comment on the image-driven platitudinous and profoundly dishonest nature of mainstream American politics. Beatty married Annette Bening after they met on the set of *Bugsy* and he has lived down his womanizing reputation.

ABOVE *Warren Beatty has fought hard to establish his credibility as an actor and a radical film-maker in the face of massive publicity about his private life.*

GENE HACKMAN (b. 1930)

Hackman's first important movie was *Bonnie and Clyde* (1967), and he also gave a fine performance in the underrated *I Never Sang for My Father*. However, it was with *The French Connection* (1971) that he achieved real stardom in a performance for which he won the Best Actor Oscar. Coppola's *The Conversation* was another high point in the actor's blossoming career. Thereafter, his career levelled off and he took too many routine roles in some poorish movies – *No Way Out, Mississippi Burning, Unforgiven* and *Absolute Power* were perhaps the best of them. Hollywood seems to have found it hard to find rewarding parts for Hackman, but he shone as the roguish lawyer father in *The Royal Tenenbaums* (2001).

ABOVE *Gene Hackman made an immense impact in his memorable role as tough detective Popeye Doyle on the trail of drug barons in* The French Connection *(1971).*

JACK NICHOLSON (b. 1937)

If "streetwise" describes Nicholson's screen persona in his earlier films, the adjective "demonic" would certainly have to be added in relation to his later films. Nicholson had small parts in some of Roger Corman's horror films of the early 1960s and then had a huge success as the alienated and drug-addicted lawyer in *Easy Rider*. In *Five Easy Pieces*, *Carnal Knowledge* and *The King of Marvin Gardens* Nicholson played loners imbued with self-dislike, alienated from their roots and out of touch with their feelings. A succession of "streetwise" roles followed in *The Last Detail*, *Chinatown*, *Tommy*, *One Flew Over the Cuckoo's Nest*, *The Missouri Breaks* and *The Last Tycoon*. His demonic side first appeared in *The Shining*, was reprised in part in *Terms of Endearment* and replayed in full for *The Witches of Eastwick*. He played a homeless bum in *Ironweed*, stole *Batman* as an over-the-top comic villain, reprised his *Chinatown* role in *The Two Jakes* (he also directed the movie), took the title role of *Hoffa*, has twice acted under Sean Penn's direction in *The Crossing Guard* and *The Pledge*, and won an Oscar for his comedy role in *As Good As It Gets* (1997). Yet, his best performances were in the early 1970s when he seemed to symbolize the restless alienation and cynicism of Nixon's America.

ABOVE *Jack Nicholson as the streetwise but ultimately bemused private eye in Roman Polanski's homage to* film noir, Chinatown. *When Nicholson is good on screen, he is very, very good. When he is bad...*

LEFT *Tony Curtis as Sydney Falco in* Sweet Smell of Success. *Burt Lancaster as the corrupt columnist J.J. Hunsecker says to Falco, "You're a cookie full of arsenic", and he sees to it that the streetwise press agent gets his comeuppance.*

AL PACINO (b. 1940)

Of New York-Sicilian descent, Pacino became a major star after *The Godfather* and *The Godfather Part II*, playing Michael Corleone. He has balanced powerful roles as a Mafia chieftain with a penchant for outsider parts, such as in *Scarecrow* and *Dog Day Afternoon*. He has played a lawyer defending no hopers in *And Justice for All* and a cop who blows the whistle on police corruption in *Serpico*. His aura of suppressed violence was used in *Cruising* and *Scarface*, while a softer, more humane face was revealed in *Bobby Deerfield* and *Author! Author!* He won an Oscar for his role in *Scent of a Woman* (1992), but he was far better in *Glengarry Glen Ross* in the same year. Among the big movies he made in the 1990s, *Carlito's Way*, *City Hall*, *Donnie Brasco*, *The Insider* and *Heat* stand out.

MICHAEL DOUGLAS (b. 1944)

Son of Kirk Douglas, Michael first came to prominence in the television cop series *The Streets of San Francisco*. Being second-generation Hollywood

LEFT *Al Pacino first made an impression in* The Godfather *(1972) and then followed that up with an impressive performance in the 1974 sequel* The Godfather Part II.

probably gave him an early insight into the movie business and he followed in his father's footsteps by becoming a major star, but he also became a producer. He co-produced *One Flew Over the Cuckoo's Nest* and then achieved success as an actor in *Coma*, *The China Syndrome*, *Romancing the Stone* and *A Chorus Line*. In 1987 he really hit the jackpot with two major hits, *Fatal Attraction*, where he played an errant husband who pays heavily for his adultery with Glenn Close, and *Wall Street*, in which he played a very rich but unscrupulous dealer in junk bonds. In *The War of the Roses* he was again in the midst of marital trouble. In the 1990s *Basic Instinct*, *Falling Down*, *Disclosure*, *The American President*, *The Game* and *A Perfect Murder* were a string of hits for Douglas. A change of pace and style for his worn-down academic role in *Wonder Boys* did his reputation no harm and *Traffic* further enhanced it. He married Welsh star Catherine Zeta-Jones in 2000.

JEFF BRIDGES (b. 1949)

Son of Lloyd Bridges, Jeff's first major film was *The Last Picture Show*, directed by Peter Bogdanovich. He often plays charming rogues as in *Bad Company*, *Thunderbolt and Lightfoot* and *Stay Hungry*. That charm can also be used to suggest hidden pathological intent as in *Jagged Edge* and *The Morning After*. *The Fabulous Baker Boys* was a hit for Bridges and his brother Beau. *Fearless* and *The Big Lebowski* were two of the better movies Bridges made in the 1990s.

ABOVE *Michael Douglas found himself in trouble with the female sex again in the highly successful but dubious* Basic Instinct *(1992).*

RIGHT The Fabulous Baker Boys (1989) *featured real-life brothers Jeff and Beau Bridges as a piano-playing night-club act, with Michelle Pfeiffer as their glamorous singer.*

RICHARD GERE (b. 1949)

Gere came to prominence with *Days of Heaven* and *Yanks*. His good looks and the impression of overt narcissism were used to good effect in *American Gigolo* and *An Officer and a Gentleman*, the latter confirming his star status. A series of failed films (*Breathless*, *The Cotton Club*, *King David* and *No Mercy*) did his career no good, but *Internal Affairs* and *Pretty Woman* were hits for him. *Final Analysis*, *Sommersby*, *Intersection* and *First Knight* were among the so-so movies Gere made in the 90s.

61

ABOVE *Richard Gere plays sensitive in* Sommersby *(1993), which was a Hollywood remake of the French movie,* The Return of Martin Guerre. *Gere too often comes over on screen as immensely self-satisfied and vain, but he still retains a legion of mainly female fans.*

ABOVE *Nicolas Cage in leopard-skin jacket as Sailor Ripley in David Lynch's* Wild at Heart *(1990).*

NICOLAS CAGE (b. 1964)

Nicolas Cage has gradually become a major star in Hollywood, his status confirmed by his 1995 Oscar for his portrayal of an alcoholic in *Leaving Las Vegas*. He is famous for his brooding intensity, apparent in films such as *Wild at Heart*, but he is equally successful in more sensitive roles such as the soft-hearted policeman in the gentle comedy *It Could Happen to You*. He has the credentials to succeed in Tinsel Town; his uncle is Francis Ford Coppola and he has been married to Patricia Arquette and Lisa Marie Presley. However, his talent and screen presence more than surpass his background and he remains one of the most impressive stars of his generation. Not all his choices of movies have been wise, however. *The Rock*, *Con Air* and *Face/Off* were all forgettable, but *Bringing Out the Dead* (1999) and *Adaptation* (2002) restored his reputation.

KEVIN SPACEY (b. 1959)

Spacey is one of the most talented actors to emerge from Hollywood since the early 1990s. He is, however, much more than a movie star, which he proves by returning to the stage from time to time to take on important dramatic roles, for example in *The Iceman Cometh*. He first made an impact on screen in *Glengarry Glen Ross*, then really made star status with his role in *The Usual Suspects* (1995). He followed this with his performance as the deranged serial

ABOVE *Kevin Spacey as the glacial Williamson with Jack Lemmon as the loser salesman Levene in the 1992 movie version of David Mamet's play* Glengarry Glen Ross.

killer in *Seven*, his corrupt detective in *L.A. Confidential* a couple of years later and a cold Hollywood wheeler-dealer in *Hurly-Burly*. He finally won an Oscar for his leading role in *American Beauty*. He has a tremendous presence on screen, but what he has to guard against is repeating too often the "Kevin Spacey" performance – that sardonic, cynical, coldly detached persona that he does so well.

DENZEL WASHINGTON (b. 1954)

Washington first made a real impression when he played South African activist Steve Biko in *Cry Freedom* (1987). He also triumphed in *Glory*, *Mo' Better Blues* (directed by

ABOVE *Denzel Washington is hired to trace a missing woman in the stylish homage to film noir,* Devil in a Blue Dress *(1995). The picture was directed by Carl Franklin.*

Spike Lee) and as Malcolm X in the 1992 Lee-directed movie of that name. He was an honourable private eye in *Devil in a Blue Dress* and an American soldier in *Courage Under Fire*. Washington can play tough and cynical, but mostly he is cast as the good guy, although ironically he won the Best Actor Oscar in 2002 for playing a corrupt cop in *Training Day*. He had given much better performances in much better movies, but Hollywood had decided it was time to award a black American actor the top male acting award and Denzel fitted the bill that year.

THE TOUGH GUYS

JAMES CAGNEY (1899–1986)

Cagney played a succession of gangster roles in movies such as *The Public Enemy* (1931), *Jimmy the Gent* (1934), *Angels with Dirty Faces* (1938) and *The Roaring Twenties* (1939). So convincing was he in these roles that much of his fan mail reputedly came from men in prison. Cagney could never have been accused of underplaying in these roles, but the lack of subtlety in his acting style did not seem to worry his legion of fans. In between these gangster pictures, he displayed his dancing skills in *Footlight Parade* (1933) and he even appeared bizarrely as Bottom in *A Midsummer Night's Dream* (1935). He was identified with rather mindless action flicks as well, including *The Crowd Roars* (1932), *The St Louis Kid* (1934), *Devil Dogs of the Air* (1935) and *Each Dawn I Die* (1939). However, Cagney continually chafed against type-casting and proved his point by winning an Oscar for his portrayal of Irish-American hoofer George M. Cohan in *Yankee Doodle Dandy* (1942). He was curiously unsuited to western roles and bombed in *The Oklahoma Kid* (1939) and *Tribute to a Bad Man* (1956). The last good gangster role he had was in Raoul Walsh's 1949 *White Heat*, in which he played a mother-fixated psychopath ("Top of the world, Ma!"). The 1950s were not particularly kind to Cagney: only *Mister Roberts* (1955), *Love Me or Leave Me* (1955) and *Man of a Thousand Faces* (1957) in which he

RIGHT *John Wayne began to be taken seriously after starring in the 1939 John Ford western* Stagecoach. *After this movie, Wayne was a Grade A star.*

played Lon Chaney Senior, made any kind of impact. Thereafter, his career went into decline, although he made one last movie appearance in the 1981 *Ragtime*. Cagney was one of those actors who disdained the profession that brought them fame and wealth; but his power and cockiness on screen, where he dominated the frame in a succession of psychopathic roles, won him a huge following. Cagney snarling "You dirty rat!" is an essential part of any mimic's repertoire.

JOHN WAYNE (1907–79)

For some reason known as "The Duke", Wayne evoked strong responses among movie-goers and non-movie-goers alike. Fans loved him for his stature and presence on screen; detracters hated him for his over-emphatic macho image and his extreme right-wing views. No one could deny his box-office impact, however; after *Stagecoach* (1939) established him as a star, he became

ABOVE *George Raft (1895–1980) was one of Cagney and Bogart's great rivals for meaty gangster roles. The logic of this is debatable, though, because he was as wooden an actor as they come. Perhaps his real-life connections with the Mafia did him no harm.*

Hollywood's most bankable asset in a succession of movies, most of which were far from memorable. His best

work was done for two directors: John Ford and Howard Hawks. Ford directed him in *Stagecoach*, *The Long Voyage Home*, *Three Godfathers*, *Fort Apache*, *She Wore a Yellow Ribbon*, *Rio Grande*, *The Quiet Man*, *The Searchers*, *The Man Who Shot Liberty Valance* and *Donovan's Reef*; Hawks directed him in *Red River*, *Rio Bravo* and *El Dorado*. Wayne won an Oscar for his role as Rooster Cogburn in *True Grit*, but it is the movies he made with Ford and Hawks that he will be remembered for.

Wayne's political views led him to support the persecution of liberals and lefties in Hollywood during the McCarthyite investigations. There was even talk of his standing as Goldwater's vice-presidential candidate in the 1964 election, but that might not now appear any more risible than the fact that America twice elected Ronald Reagan as president!

HUMPHREY BOGART
(1899–1957)

Bogart, or "Bogey", has a cult status close to that of Monroe and Dean. He symbolized the tough guy with integrity, the kind of guy whom you'd want around if things turned ugly, but on whom you could also count to do the decent thing. These characteristics made him a natural for the part of Philip Marlowe in *The Big Sleep* and Sam Spade in *The Maltese Falcon*. His role as Rick in *Casablanca* also reflected the "Bogey" persona: tough, cynical, worldly but with a heart of gold under that veneer of nihilism. When Woody Allen is having difficulties with women in *Play It Again, Sam* he turns to Bogart (or an actor impersonating Bogey) for advice, which naturally leads to successs with the ladies.

The Bogart persona is a favourite with most professional and amateur impersonators. Dressed in a shabby raincoat, with the ever-present cigarette, the Bogey imitator usually does an abbreviated version of his

ABOVE *One of Humphrey Bogart's most memorable gangster roles was in the 1941 Raoul Walsh-directed* High Sierra, *adapted from a W.R. Burnett novel.*

speeches in the famous last scene of *Casablanca*: "It doesn't take a genius to figure that the problems of three little people don't amount to a hill of beans in this crazy world..." Bogart was married four times. His last marriage to Lauren Bacall, with whom he made *To Have and Have Not*, *The Big Sleep* and *Key Largo*, was by far the most successful relationship. Happiness with Bacall coincided with later film triumphs such as the Oscar he won for his role in *The African Queen* and his performance as Captain Queeg in *The Caine Mutiny*. However, cancer cut short his life in 1957, probably because of the accumulative effect of too much smoking and drinking. But the Bogart persona lives on.

RIGHT *Edward G. Robinson was an actor with a much wider range than tough guy roles allowed him to display. Here he appears as the kindly patriarch in* Our Vines Have Tender Grapes *(1945), co-starring Margaret O'Brien and Agnes Moorhead.*

ALAN LADD (1913–64)

Ladd became a star after *This Gun for Hire* (1942); his co-star was Veronica Lake, and he went on to make *The Glass Key* and *The Blue Dahlia* with her. Raymond Chandler wrote that Ladd was a small boy's idea of a tough guy, and certainly Ladd suffered from "sizist" jokes because of his diminutive stature. But at the peak of his career he was enormously popular – partly because of his brooding choirboy features, which suggested imminent violence. His best part was Shane in the western of the same name.

BELOW *In the 1954 western* Drum Beat *Alan Ladd plays the role of an Indian expert, Johnny MacKay, who tries to be understanding to Charles Bronson, an Apache chief called Captain Jack. The movie attempted to recapture the west authentically.*

RIGHT *In* The Blue Dahlia *(1946), Alan Ladd plays a returning GI suspected of murder. His death was a result of pills and booze. Whether this was intentional or accidental is not known.*

Despite this huge success, Ladd continued to feel insecure, and he became an alcoholic. He died in 1964 at the age of 51, having consumed a cocktail of alcohol and sedatives. In *Rebel Without a Cause* there is a scene where the tiny teenager Sal Mineo opens his high-school locker and we see a picture of Alan Ladd stuck on the inside of the locker door. Yes, indeed, a small boy's idea of a tough guy.

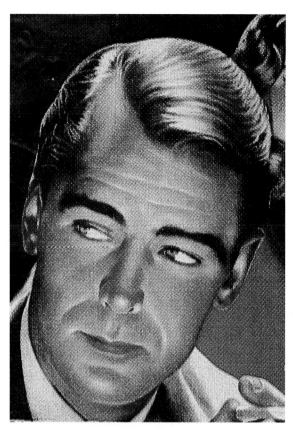

BURT LANCASTER (1913–94)

Lancaster is hard to categorize but many of his roles have involved him in "tough guy" antics. His first film *The Killers* (1946) had him as an ex-gangster waiting stoically for his own demise at the hands of two goons. He played a very tough guy indeed in *Brute Force*, a liberal prison movie directed by Jules Dassin. Lancaster had been a circus acrobat before becoming an actor and he employed these talents in the swashbucklers *The Flame and the Arrow* and *The Crimson Pirate*. But he always sought to play a broad range of parts and this is reflected in the variety of movies he made in the 1950s: *From Here to Eternity, Come Back Little Sheba, The Rainmaker, Vera Cruz, Sweet Smell of Success, Gunfight at the OK Corral* and

Separate Tables. He followed these with *Birdman of Alcatraz* and *The Leopard,* which was directed by Luchino Visconti, the Italian director with a penchant for operatic effects.

Thrillers such as *Seven Days in May* and *Executive Action* suggest Lancaster's politics leant towards the liberal, and he was always interested in playing people from ethnic minorities, such as *Apache, Jim Thorpe – All-American* and *Valdez is Coming*. He had two successes in the 1980s: *Atlantic City* and *Local Hero*. He also played Moses for television, and so Lancaster, if he was a tough-guy actor, was certainly a versatile tough guy. He will always be remembered for his role as the cynical and corrupt newspaper columnist in *Sweet Smell of Success.*

ABOVE *Burt Lancaster as J.J. Hunsecker, a poisonous newspaper columnist in one of the best Hollywood movies of the 1950s,* Sweet Smell of Success *(1957).*

KIRK DOUGLAS (b. 1916)

Douglas was at one time dubbed "the most hated man in Hollywood" because of his reputation for aggressiveness and egomania. Another jibe thrown at him was that he has always wanted to be Burt Lancaster. Certainly their careers have often coincided (*Gunfight at the OK Corral, The Devil's Disciple, The List of Adrian Messenger, Seven Days in May* and *Tough Guys*). Douglas's forte is portraying obsessed, self-destructive loners, which he proved in films such as *Champion, Ace in the Hole, Detective*

ABOVE *Steve McQueen loved doing his own stunts. In* The Great Escape *(1963) he fled from the German Gestapo by motorbike.*

Story, *The Bad and the Beautiful, Lust for Life* (as Vincent Van Gogh) and *Two Weeks in Another Town*. But he has also played various larger-than-life heroic roles, in particular in *Spartacus, Twenty Thousand Leagues Under the Sea, Paths of Glory, In Harm's Way* and *Cast a Giant Shadow*. His best part? Not everyone will agree, but my vote for this goes to his role in *Lust for Life*. Even after a series of strokes hampered his speech and movement, he fought back to continue acting in small parts.

STEVE MCQUEEN (1930–80)

Steve McQueen was a macho star who very often insisted on doing his own stunts. In the famous car chase in *Bullitt* he drove the car himself, and in the motorbike escape section in *The Great Escape* he

ABOVE *Jan Sterling tells Kirk Douglas, "I've met some hard-boiled eggs in my time, but you're six-and-a-half minutes!" in Billy Wilder's* The Big Carnival (*aka* Ace in the Hole, *1951*).

not only rode his own motorbike but the bike of his supposed pursuer as well. McQueen had an icy quality on screen, which many people liked and which just as many disliked. But enough movie-goers flocked to his films to make him a very big star indeed. He first made an impact in the 1960 western *The Magnificent Seven*, then he made *The War Lover* (1962), *The Great Escape* (1963), *Love with the Proper Stranger* (1963), *The Cincinnati Kid* (1965) and *The Sand Pebbles* (1966). Other hits included *The Thomas Crown Affair* (1968), *Bullitt* (1968), *Le Mans* (1971), *The Getaway* (1972), *Papillon* (1973) and *The Towering Inferno* (1974). He died of cancer at the age of 50 in 1980, and retains a legion of fans.

CLINT EASTWOOD (b. 1930)

Eastwood was the major macho star of the 1960s, 70s and 80s. He made his name in the spaghetti westerns *A Fistful of Dollars, For a Few Dollars More* and *The Good, the Bad and the Ugly*. He then struck another goldmine with a series of films in which he played psychopathic cop Harry Callahan: *Dirty Harry, Magnum Force, The Enforcer, Sudden Impact* and *The Dead Pool*. In between he made action movies such as *Where Eagles Dare* and *The Eiger Sanction*. He sang disastrously in *Paint Your Wagon* but other attempts to break the Eastwood mould have been more successful, notably in *Bronco Billy* and *Honky Tonk Man*.

Eastwood's acting style belongs, as someone once said, to "the Mount Rushmore school of acting" but audiences and critics seem to approve. He has directed numerous films such as *Play Misty for Me, The Outlaw Josey Wales, Bird, White Hunter, Black Heart* and *Unforgiven* (for which he won the Best Director Oscar). He has continued to

ABOVE *Clint Eastwood played the vigilante cop Dirty Harry in the third movie of the series* The Enforcer (1976).

act and direct in movies such as *In the Line of Fire, The Bridges of Madison County, Absolute Power, Midnight in the Garden of Good and Evil, Space Cowboys, Blood Work* and *Million Dollar Baby* (for which he won his second Director Oscar and was nominated for his performance).

SYLVESTER STALLONE (b. 1946)

Stallone has specialized in characters whose biceps are bigger than their brains. His first and greatest success was with *Rocky*, which he wrote for himself to star in. Another "character" Stallone has spawned is Rambo, a vigilante who murdered hundreds in his three films. Declining audiences for his movies forced him to reassess, and he tried a gentler role in *Cop Land*, a role for which he was over-praised. What do aging musclebound stars do? They usually make movies that parody their former screen personas. Watch this space.

RIGHT *Stallone's first big success was in* Rocky (1976) *playing a no-hoper boxer who gets a shot at the title against all the odds.*

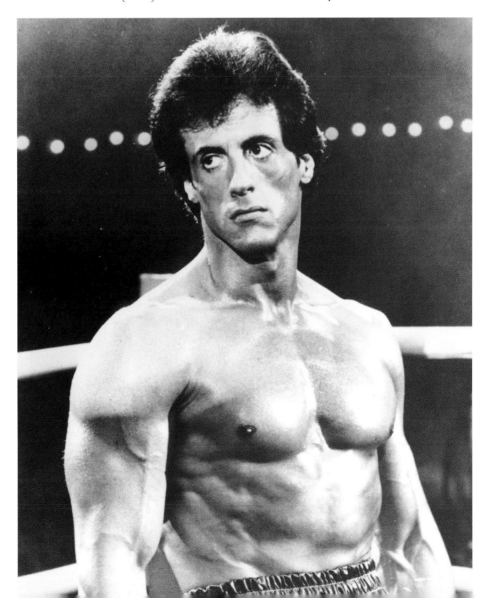

ABOVE *Schwarzenegger hands out the kind of arbitrary justice that his screen characters seem to indulge in, this time as the avenging angel in* The Last Action Hero *(1993).*

ARNOLD SCHWARZENEGGER (b. 1947)

Schwarzenegger was a Mr Universe before he started "acting". His first films featured him in his real-life role as a muscle-man: *Stay Hungry* and *Pumping Iron*, but soon he was playing roles such as *Conan the Barbarian* and *Conan the Destroyer*. *The Terminator*, *Commando*, *Red Sonja*, *Raw Deal*, *Predator* and *Total Recall* made him the favourite of the Saturday-night-video-and-takeaway circuit. He was also encouraged to show off his softer side in the truly cynical *Kindergarten Cop*. He is not as mindless as his roles might suggest; he was in the comedy *Twins*, with Danny De Vito playing his unlikely twin. His career and the box-office returns from his movies have zoomed downwards since the mid-1990s. Married to one of the Kennedy clan, Schwarzenegger was always rumoured to have political ambitions, and in 2003 he was elected Governor of California.

MEL GIBSON (b. 1956)

Gibson (born of American parents but spending his formative years in Australia) first came to prominence in the *Mad Max* movies, which helped to put him and the new Australian cinema on the movie map. He was also very effective in Peter Weir's *Gallipoli* and *The Year of Living Dangerously*, and in the Fletcher Christian part in *The Bounty*. However, the movies that really catapulted him to world stardom were the *Lethal Weapon* quartet. Teamed with Danny Glover, Gibson starred as a flaky detective prone to self-destruction in these action movies that make few demands on the brain cells. *Bird on a*

BELOW *Mel Gibson as he appeared in the* Lethal Weapon *series.*

Wire with Goldie Hawn flopped at the box office, but there is no doubt that Gibson was now established as a major world star. He has also made a successful transition into a star/director role, firstly with *The Man Without a Face* and in the Oscar-winning *Braveheart*. He also played Hamlet in the 1990 Franco Zeffirelli version of the Shakespeare play. Critics on the whole were kind to him, but this did not encourage him to pitch for more serious roles. *The Patriot* was called stridently anti-British by British critics and won him few friends. *What Women Want* raised the hackles of feminists, *Signs* was another hit for him, and his writing, producing and directing of *The Passion of the Christ* (2004) aroused major religious controversy all over the world. Gibson is probably a better actor than most of his film roles allow him to be.

BRUCE WILLIS (b. 1955)

Willis gives the impression on screen of being inordinately pleased with himself. Even when he is playing

modest and shy, somehow it smacks of narcissism. The no-brainer *Die Hard* (1988) was a huge hit and really launched Willis into stardom; there have been sequels. He had an absolute disaster with *Hudson Hawk*, which might have stalled his career, but *Pulp Fiction*, *Twelve Monkeys*, *The Fifth Element* and *The Siege* brought it back on track. In *The Sixth Sense* and *Unbreakable*, he took on more vulnerable roles. For a number of years during the 1990s, Willis and his then-wife Demi Moore were seen as

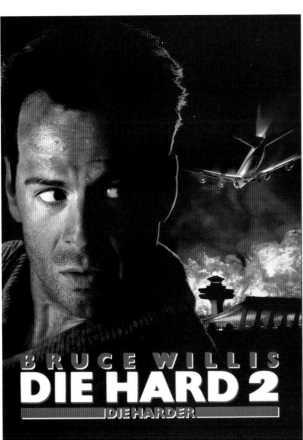

LEFT Die Harder *was the unsubtle tagline for the second of the* Die Hard *movies that made Bruce Willis a star.*

ABOVE Russell Crowe first came to the notice of the wider movie public through his role in Romper Stomper, *an Australian film about racist skinheads directed by Geoffrey Wright.*

Hollywood's golden couple, which may or may not say something about Hollywood of that era.

RUSSELL CROWE (b. 1964)

Crowe is a New Zealander who started his acting career in Australian television soaps. Two notable Australian movies he made were *Proof* (1991) and *Romper Stomper* (1992). He gravitated to Hollywood and made the big time when he played the violent cop in *L.A. Confidential*. By contrast, he played a shy and inadequate whistle-blower in *The Insider*, before having a major triumph in *Gladiator*. He received Oscar nominations three years running with *The Insider* (1999), *Gladiator* (2000) – for which he won the Best Actor award – and *A Beautiful Mind* (2001).

LEFT *Keanu Reeves had a huge box-office hit with the out-of-control-bus thriller* Speed, *which also starred Dennis Hopper and Sandra Bullock.*

KEANU REEVES (b. 1964)

Reeves became something of a cult figure with young audiences after movies such *Bill and Ted's Excellent Adventure*, *Point Break* and *My Own Private Idaho*, but it was in action movies such as *Speed*, *Chain Reaction* and *The Matrix* trilogy that he gained his largest audiences. For many, his appeal remains a matter of mystery.

SAMUEL L. JACKSON (b. 1948)

Jackson was in Spike Lee's *Do the Right Thing* and *Jungle Fever*, as well as Scorsese's *GoodFellas*. It was his part in Tarantino's *Pulp Fiction* that finally established his screen persona as the tough guy, and he was also in that director's *Jackie Brown*. However, he is an actor with a fairly wide range and he has played different kinds of roles in *Trees Lounge* and *The Red Violin*, a movie that deserves to find a wider audience. Jackson is mostly used in actioners, but as he gets older, I would expect him to be cast more and more in parts that exploit his intelligence and fluency as an actor.

Jackson is one of Hollywood's growing number of major black stars, a trail blazed by Sidney Poitier and Dorothy Dandridge in the 1950s. He has a more powerful screen presence than Poitier, a wider acting range, and is certainly not as tied to dignified black roles as Poitier was.

ABOVE *Samuel L. Jackson played a character called Zeus (no, not God!) in* Die Hard with a Vengeance. *He has had more thoughtful roles, notably alongside Greta Scacchi and Don McKellar in* The Red Violin *and in* Trees Lounge, *directed by fellow actor Steve Buscemi.*

THE COMEDY ACTORS

Comedy actors are a different breed from comics like Chaplin and Keaton. Comedy actors are not really professional clowns, they play ordinary people who find themselves in difficulties, and the comedy arises as they try to extricate themselves from their predicaments. Comedy is a real test of an actor: think of Laurence Olivier – he was a brilliant comic actor and he usually brought a comic element even to tragic roles.

WILLIAM POWELL (1892–1984)

Debonair is the adjective most over-used about Powell, but he was an accomplished comedy actor in movies such as *My Man Godfrey*, *Love Crazy*, *Life with Father*, and in the *Thin Man* series with co-star Myrna Loy.

CAROLE LOMBARD (1908–42)

Lombard was an intelligent, tough comedy actress who was killed in an air crash in 1942, leaving Clark Gable a widower. She showed her prowess in *Twentieth Century*, *My Man Godfrey*, *Nothing Sacred*, *They Knew What They Wanted*, *Mr and Mrs Smith* and *To Be or Not to Be*.

ROSALIND RUSSELL (1908–76)

Russell was at her best in comedies such as *The Women*, *His Girl Friday*, *My Sister Eileen* and *The Velvet Touch*. She also played dramatic roles in *Night Must Fall*, *Sister Kenny* and *Picnic*. She was the screen's Auntie Mame.

CARY GRANT (1904–86)

British-born Archie Leach became Cary Grant and went on to establish himself as one of Hollywood's greatest stars. Picked by Mae West for *She Done Him Wrong* (1933), Grant was soon in demand as a comedy actor in movies such as *The Awful Truth*, *Bringing Up Baby*, *His Girl Friday* and *The Philadelphia Story*. His dark, good looks also qualified him for straight roles in *Gunga Din*, *Only Angels Have*

ABOVE *Alastair Sim (1900–76) was one of the most accomplished movie comedy actors. Here he appears as the headmistress in* The Belles of St Trinian's *(1954).*

Wings and *Suspicion* – the latter directed by Hitchcock who saw something more sinister behind those handsome features, which he exploited later in *Notorious*. Other important comedies were *I Was a Male War Bride*, *Monkey Business* and *Operation Petticoat*, which he mixed with straight roles in *North by Northwest*, *An Affair to Remember*, *Indiscreet* and *Charade*. Grant symbolized sophistication for many film-goers, but he was not afraid to show himself as ridiculous in his comedies. Married five times, Grant retired from movies in 1966 to devote himself to promoting cosmetics for an internationally known firm. He died at the age of 82 in 1986 after weathering the passage of time remarkably well.

ABOVE *Carole Lombard as she appeared in Ernet Lubitsch's* To Be or Not to Be *(1942). Lombard was one of the best comedy actresses Hollywood has ever produced.*

ABOVE *Cary Grant in drag in the Howard Hawks comedy* I Was a Male War Bride.

LEFT *One of Jack Lemmon's best screen roles was in Billy Wilder's* The Apartment, *in which he played an ambitious New York "Organization Man" willing to lend out his apartment to his philandering bosses.*

JACK LEMMON (1925–2002)

Lemmon was often accused of working too hard at the comic effects he aimed to achieve, and certainly he could never be said to underplay, but he was very effective in some movies such as *Some Like it Hot*, *The Apartment*, *How to Murder Your Wife*, *The Fortune Cookie*, *The Odd Couple* and *The Front Page*. Lemmon was particularly associated in the public's mind with characters in Neil Simon comedies such as *The Out-of-Towners* and *The Prisoner of Second Avenue*. In these movies he played the harassed American middle-class male, beset by problems of urban violence, bureaucratic red tape and the general hassle of 20th-century life. He also played straight roles in *Days of Wine* and *Roses*, *Save the Tiger*, *The China Syndrome*, *Missing* and *JFK*. His irresistible bantering relationship with co-star Walter Matthau in *The Odd Couple* was reprised in two *Grumpy Old Men* movies in the 1990s. Lemmon's speciality was the decent, average middle-class man all at sea in a world of dishonesty and brutality.

WALTER MATTHAU (1920–2000)

Born Walter Matthow, the son of Jewish-Russian immigrants to New York, Matthau achieved star status comparatively late in life. His

GRUMPY OLD MEN

ABOVE *Both Jack Lemmon and Walter Matthau indulged in misogynistic roles from time to time in movies such as* How To Murder Your Wife *(1965).*

ABOVE *Peter Sellers had a great popular success in the series of* Pink Panther *movies, playing the hapless Inspector Clouseau.*

speciality was the cynical slob, and he played variations on this stereotype in *The Fortune Cookie, The Odd Couple, Plaza Suite, Kotch, The Sunshine Boys, The Bad News Bears, House Calls* and *California Suite.* He also played assorted villains in various movies and had the misfortune to play opposite Streisand in *Hello Dolly!* His critical and sarcastic comments about her indicated that his on-screen persona reflected a lot of his own personality. He directed one low-budget picture, *Gangster Story* in 1960.

PETER SELLERS (1925–80)

Sellers made his name in *The Goon Show* on British radio, then graduated to British movies such as *The Ladykillers, The Smallest Show on Earth, I'm All Right, Jack* and *Only Two Can Play.* When he went to Hollywood, his early films such as

OPPOSITE *Good friends Lemmon and Matthau appeared in* Grumpy Old Men *(1993), a success for both actors late in their screen careers.*

Lolita, Dr Strangelove (in which he played three parts) and *The Pink Panther* held promise of a great international career. But his emotional problems and a disastrous run of bad films put his career into reverse. A near-fatal heart attack in 1964 seemed to increase his sour view of life, but he found steady work and success in the series of Inspector Clouseau films that followed *The Pink Panther* after a ten-year gap – although they scarcely stretched him as a comedy actor. One last worthwhile film before he finally succumbed to his heart condition was *Being There* (1979). Sellers once said revealingly, "If you ask me to play myself, I will not know what to do. I do not know who or what I am." Sellers was a man who hid behind funny voices.

DANNY DEVITO (b. 1944)

Of diminutive stature, DeVito became a major comedy star in the 1980s in movies such as *Ruthless People, Wise Guys, Throw Momma from the Train, Twins, Tin Men, The War of the Roses* and *Other People's Money.* He was in *Batman Returns* and acted in and directed *Hoffa.* In the 1990s he remained a very busy actor; among the movies he acted in were *Get Shorty, Mars Attacks, L.A. Confidential* and *The Virgin Suicides.* He is quoted as saying that a person of his height and looks is forced to cultivate immense self-esteem and confidence, otherwise they would go under in a society that worships good looks and suavity.

75

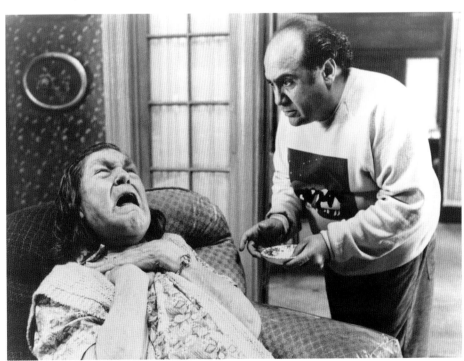

ABOVE *Danny DeVito, seen here with co-star Anne Ramsey, had a major success in the misanthropic comedy* Throw Momma from the Train *(1987).*

LEFT *Robin Williams played perhaps the quintessential Robin Williams role in* Hook *as Peter Pan, the boy who never really grew up to be a man.*

of the Williams screen persona so he appeared as psychotics in *Insomnia* and *One Hour Photo*, which revealed him as an actor who can convey sinister depths. Let us hope he pursues this side of his talent as he goes into his 50s rather than the clownish kid aspect of his screen persona. Let the real Robin Williams stand up.

BEN STILLER (b. 1965)

Stiller is better known as a comic actor than as a director, but he has directed *Reality Bites* (1994), *The Cable Guy* (1996) and *Zoolander* (2001). As an actor he won a huge following after his success in the gross-out comedy *There's Something About Mary* (1998), but *Mystery Men* (1999) did not enhance his career much. He was amusing as the put-upon potential son-in-law Greg Focker in the hit film *Meet the Parents* (2000), and played Chas the international real estate whizz in *The Royal Tenenbaums* (2001).

ROBIN WILLIAMS (b. 1952)

Williams started out as a stand-up comedian, then went into the television series *Mork and Mindy*, which brought him fame and fortune and opened the door to Hollywood. His first really big hit was *Good Morning, Vietnam*, which was followed by *Dead Poets Society*. Both roles represented Williams as a life force bringing enlightenment into other people's lives. This has been the most irritating part of the Williams persona, that and the unending need to be loved by audiences. *Mrs Doubtfire* was another hit for the actor, but along the way he made some turkeys as well. His career reached a nadir with the quite nauseating *Patch Adams*. He must have realized he needed new direction because the public were clearly tiring

ABOVE *Ben Stiller shakes Robert De Niro's hand in* Meet the Parents (2000). *De Niro's character, an ex-CIA agent, has his prospective son-in-law investigated to see if he's up to scratch.*

THREE GREAT STARS

Marlon Brando, George C. Scott and Robert De Niro qualify for the accolade of all-time greats but they defy categorization, although some critics have tried to pigeon-hole them into certain sterotypes.

MARLON BRANDO (1924–2004)

Born in 1924 in Omaha, Nebraska, Brando played Stanley Kowalski in *A Streetcar Named Desire* on Broadway before starring in Elia Kazan's film version. This part created the Brando stereotype: the incoherent, primitive and rapacious male animal. However, the tabloids who peddled that stereotype conveniently ignored the range of parts that the "Method" actor undertook: the paraplegic in *The Men*

ABOVE *Marlon Brando as Don Corleone hears a plea for help from the local undertaker in* The Godfather *(1972).*

(1950), his first movie, the Mexican revolutionary in *Viva Zapata*, Mark Antony in *Julius Caesar* and the motorbike gang leader in *The Wild One*. His most memorable part in the early part of his film career was in *On the Waterfront*. Again he played an incoherent, potentially violent man, but Brando revealed reserves of tenderness and vulnerability in the character, thereby creating one of the all-time great screen performances.

Brando never really hid his contempt for his profession; perhaps his hatred was reserved more for the business end of the film business than for film acting itself, but his lack of care led him into making some movie stinkers, including *Desirée*, *The Teahouse of the August Moon*, *Sayonara*,

LEFT *Marlon Brando (Marc Antony) emotes over the dead body of Caesar while James Mason (Brutus) addresses the Roman mob in the 1953 production* Julius Caesar.

Bedtime Story and *Candy*. But his range was staggering: from Shakespeare to musicals, from drama to comedies. He was a charming Sky Masterson in *Guys and Dolls* and an effete Fletcher Christian in *Mutiny on the Bounty*. It was *Bounty* that marked a break with the Hollywood moguls who complained about long delays in the shooting of the film because of Brando's whims. He directed *One-Eyed Jacks* in 1960, starred in *The Chase* and *Reflections in a Golden Eye* in the 60s, the only two decent movies he made in that decade, and then appeared as Don Corleone in *The Godfather* in 1972. When the Academy awarded him an Oscar, he sent a Native American woman to collect it in order to draw attention to the plight of contemporary Native Americans in the USA. Increasingly Brando devoted himself to causes, and his later films reflected his political leanings: *Queimada*, *Roots: the New Generation* (for television), *Apocalypse Now*, *The Formula* and *A Dry White Season*. He had to deal with major traumas in his family life – including murder and suicide – but he continued to work in movies from time to time during the 1990s, none of them in any way memorable. "Acting is a useless and empty profession", Brando has

ABOVE *George C. Scott as fight promoter Gloves Malloy confers with director Stanley Donen in the amusing spoof of 1930s movies* Movie Movie *(1978).*

been quoted as saying. He may or may not have been right about that, but such an attitude prevented him from achieving the heights he might have done.

GEORGE C. SCOTT (1926–99)

Scott was another great screen actor with something approaching contempt for his profession. His self-loathing, by his own testimony, brought him to the brink of total breakdown on numerous occasions and he had to fight periods when he just wanted to lose himself in a bottle. Yet on screen he was one of the most powerful presences ever seen because he had that quality of being like a coiled spring just about to release the rage that boiled under the surface.

LEFT *George C. Scott won an Oscar for his role as General Patton in* Patton *(1970). He later played Benito Mussolini in a 1985 TV series* Mussolini: The Untold Story.

He was first noticed as the prosecutor in *Anatomy of a Murder*, but really made his mark as the smooth but ruthless gangster in *The Hustler*. As the cold manipulator of the pool hustler Fast Eddie (Paul Newman), Scott excelled in Robert Rossen's fine movie. Scott's range as an actor was reflected in his comic portrayal of Buck Turgidson in *Dr Strangelove*, one of his greatest screen performances. One of the real tests of actors is whether or not they can play comedy convincingly – Olivier could, but Brando never showed that he was as good in comedy as he was in dramatic roles. Scott, however, played comedy brilliantly both on screen and on stage. A series of indifferent movies followed *The Hustler*, but Scott hit the jackpot again with his portrayal of George S. Patton in *Patton* (1970). Awarded an Oscar, he refused the honour, stating that he disagreed with actors being judged in competition with one another. This might have arisen from his deep disappointment from losing out for the Best Supporting Actor Oscar when he had first been nominated for *Anatomy of a Murder*, but whatever the reason, he stuck to his guns, which inevitably did not endear him to the Hollywood establishment. Solid performances in *The Last Run* and *The Hospital* followed, but again Scott seemed fairly indifferent to the movies he appeared in. *The Day of the Dolphin, Islands in the Stream* and *Movie Movie* were the best of the 1970s. In *Movie Movie* he again showed his talent for comedy, while in Paul Schrader's *Hardcore* he played a religious man looking for his lost daughter in a pornographic underworld. Over the last 20 years of his life, he generally made fairly worthless movies, merely taking on parts to pay bills and alimony. He starred in a television movie remake of *12 Angry Men*, for which he won an Emmy award; true to form, he failed to pick up the award. The fact that he has made so few good movies is a matter of regret, but he was undoubtedly one of the most powerful screen actors that America has ever produced.

ROBERT DE NIRO (b. 1943)

De Niro first came to real prominence with his performance as Johnny Boy in Martin Scorsese's *Mean Streets*. Scorsese encouraged his actors to improvise and use aspects of their own personalities; this approach paid off, particularly in the scenes between De Niro and Harvey Keitel. Keitel and De Niro again appeared together in Scorsese's *Taxi Driver*, surely the best American film of the 1970s, and once more their improvisational technique paid dividends in terms of the realism of the scenes between them. In between these two movies, De Niro starred in *The Godfather Part II* in which he played the younger Don Corleone, Brando's part in *The Godfather*. Subtly mimicking the older actor's high-

RIGHT *De Niro played boxer Jake La Motta in Scorsese's* Raging Bull, *seen by many as De Niro's best screen performance and the director's major work.*

pitched voice from the first movie, De Niro made a convincing portrayal of the young Don Corleone learning to use the methods of his Mafia oppressors to create a comfortable life for his family.

It was appropriate that De Niro should play Corleone as a younger man because in many ways he is Brando's natural successor in Hollywood. De Niro exudes repressed and expressed violence (*Raging Bull, The Deer Hunter, Once Upon a Time in America, The Mission, The Untouchables*); he plays straight, intense, dramatic roles (*True Confessions, Angel Heart, Stanley and Iris*); he can play romantic roles (*Falling in Love*); he is also expert at comedy (*New York, New York, King of Comedy, Brazil, Midnight Run*). The actor goes to extreme lengths to prepare for his roles, for example adding 60 extra pounds to his frame to play Jake LaMotta in *Raging Bull*. It may be that, like many actors, De Niro hides from himself in the parts he plays.

In more recent years, De Niro's movies have not really extended him. Even Scorsese's *Casino* seemed to

ABOVE *Robert De Niro, Marlon Brando's heir-apparent in Hollywood, played the boxer Jake La Motta in Martin Scorsese's* Raging Bull.

demand only the retreading of familiar paths. However, he has been very successful in comedies such as *Analyze This* (1999), *Meet the Parents* (2000) and *Analyze That* (2002).

De Niro owns and helps to run a very expensive restaurant in Manhattan, and the desire to do really good work in the cinema may be draining away. At his very best, De Niro is a major acting talent.

BRITISH STARS

It may seem disproportionate to give a section over to British stars who have made it internationally, but those who appear here are difficult to categorize in terms of Hollywood archetypes. Each of them, with one exception, started in British films and then made it in Hollywood – but remained essentially British in the parts they played.

JAMES MASON (1909–84)

Mason made his name in a series of Gainsborough melodramas such as *The Man in Grey*, *The Seventh Veil* and *The Wicked Lady*. He gave a fine performance as an IRA gunman in *Odd Man Out*, then went to Hollywood and starred in *Caught*, *Pandora and the Flying Dutchman* and as Rommel in *The Desert Fox*. He was Brutus in *Julius Caesar* and the self-destructive star in *A Star is Born*, one of his finest performances. He was the villain in Hitchcock's *North by Northwest* and Humbert Humbert

in *Lolita*. Excellent performances followed in *The Pumpkin Eater*, *The Deadly Affair*, *Autobiography of a Princess* and *The Shooting Party* (1984), his last film. Mason was one of the most accomplished screen actors Britain has ever produced.

DEBORAH KERR (b. 1921)

Scots-born Kerr made *The Life and Death of Colonel Blimp*, *I See a Dark Stranger* and *Black Narcissus* before going to Hollywood and starring in *King Solomon's Mines*, *Quo Vadis*, *From Here to Eternity*, *The King and I*, *Tea and Sympathy*, *Heaven Knows, Mr Allison* and *Separate Tables*. Her most notable films after that were *The Sundowners*, *The Innocents*, *The Night of the Iguana*, *The Gypsy Moths* and *The Arrangement*. She received an Honorary Oscar for career achievement in 1994.

VIVIEN LEIGH (1913–67)

Blessed with outstanding beauty, Leigh also found her looks somewhat of a handicap when it came to being taken seriously as an actress. Married for many years to Laurence Olivier, she

ABOVE *Deborah Kerr (far left) with co-star Van Jonson on location for the 1955 version of Graham Greene's* The End of the Affair. *Too often Kerr was cast as a genteel wife, when her real talent was for earthier parts.*

ABOVE *James Mason was already a big movie star in Britain before he left for Hollywood after the war. Here is a poster for* The Night Has Eyes *(1942)*.

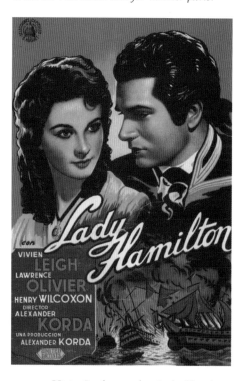

ABOVE *Vivien Leigh starred as Lady Hamilton with husband Laurence Olivier as Lord Nelson in Alexander Korda's production of* Lady Hamilton *(aka* That Hamilton Woman*)*.

ABOVE *Two of the most popular post-war British stars were Trevor Howard and Kenneth More, here seen in* The Clouded Yellow *(1950).*

BELOW *Olivier chose a 17-year-old Jean Simmons to play Ophelia to his Hamlet in the 1948 film he also directed, which won the Best Picture Oscar for that year.*

may also have suffered from being perceived as "Mrs Olivier". However, she was excellent as Scarlett O'Hara in *Gone with the Wind* and had successes with *Waterloo Bridge* and *Lady Hamilton*. Her more serious film roles in *Caesar and Cleopatra* and *Anna Karenina* did not bring her critical praise. Her last important screen role was as Blanche Dubois opposite Brando in *A Streetcar Named Desire*. After that, she made only three films: *The Deep Blue Sea*, *The Roman Spring of Mrs Stone* and *Ship of Fools*. Ill-health shortened her life and she died at the age of 54 in 1967.

TREVOR HOWARD (1916–88)

Howard had a powerful screen presence that very few other British actors have possessed. He was excellent in *Brief Encounter* and *The Third Man*, and his performances in *Outcast of the Islands* and *The Heart of the Matter* are two of the best ever in British films. He made some

Hollywood movies, notably as Captain Bligh in the Brando *Mutiny on the Bounty*, but he never became a Hollywood star. Other notable films he starred in include *Sons and Lovers*, *The Charge of the Light Brigade* and *Ryan's Daughter*. He played Pope Leo in *Pope Joan*, Richard Wagner in *Ludwig* and King Arthur in *Sword of the Valiant*.

JEAN SIMMONS (b. 1929)

Simmons's best-known British films are *Great Expectations* (as Estelle), *Black Narcissus* (as an Indian girl), *The Blue Lagoon* (shipwrecked on a desert island with Donald Houston) and *Hamlet*, Olivier choosing her to be his Ophelia. Hollywood gave her a string of mediocre parts until *Guys and Dolls*, *The Big Country*, *Elmer Gantry*, *Spartacus*

and *The Grass is Greener*. Then her career seemed to stagnate. Husbands included Stewart Granger and Richard Brooks, the director, both of whom rather domineered her. She also had a

ABOVE *One of the British movies Jean Simmons starred in before moving permanently to Hollywood was the 1950 thriller* Cage of Gold.

AUDREY HEPBURN (1929–93)

Hepburn was Belgian-born of Irish-Dutch parentage, but she ranks as a British star since she made her start in British pictures such as *Laughter in Paradise* and *The Lavender Hill Mob*. *Roman Holiday* made her a star in Hollywood and this success was followed by a string of important films: *Sabrina, War and Peace, Funny Face, The Nun's Story, Breakfast at Tiffany's, Charade* and *My Fair Lady*. She usually played child-women, an archetype that won her many ardent fans but which made it more difficult for her to get worthwhile parts in the 1970s and 80s. She played the angel Hap in *Always*, Spielberg's 1990 remake of *A Guy Named Joe*.

ABOVE *Audrey Hepburn epitomized a kind of elfin, gamin charm for her many fans. After appearing in small parts in British movies, she made it big starring with Gregory Peck in* Roman Holiday *(1953).*

long-lasting battle with the bottle. In the 1980s and 90s she made numerous television appearances, and was part of the ensemble cast of the movie *How to Make an American Quilt* (1995).

JOHN MILLS (b. 1908)

Mills never made it in Hollywood, probably because he was so irretrievably British. A succession of war movies established him as the archetypal British officer, stiff upper-lip and terribly, terribly decent: *In Which We Serve, We Dive at Dawn, The Way to the Stars, Morning Departure, The Colditz Story, Above Us the Waves, Dunkirk* and *Ice Cold in Alex*. He was also a military man in *Tunes of Glory* and *Oh! What a Lovely War*. In between war heroics, he played *Scott of the Antarctic* and Mr Polly in *The History of Mr Polly*. Hollywood movies included *War and Peace, King Rat, Ryan's Daughter* (playing a deaf mute, for which he won an Oscar for Best Supporting Actor) and *Oklahoma Crude*. But for many film fans, he will be remembered as the secret weapon the Germans never had.

Ealing Studios present another comedy: ALEC GUINNESS JOAN GREENWOOD CECIL PARKER in THE MAN IN THE WHITE SUIT

A MICHAEL BALCON PRODUCTION
DIRECTED BY ALEXANDER MACKENDRICK

DIRK BOGARDE (1921–99)

Dirk Bogarde first came to prominence as the young gunman who shoots down copper Jack Warner in *The Blue Lamp* (1948). Bogarde's employers, however, believed he had a future as a leading man and starred him in a succession of war movies such as *They Who Dare* (1953) and *The Sea Shall Not Have Them* (1954) as well as harmless comedies such as the *Doctor* series in which he played the young doctor Simon Sparrow. Bogarde played Sidney Carton in the 1958 version of *A Tale of Two Cities* and even survived playing Franz Liszt in *Song Without End* (1960). He had two successes working with director Joseph Losey: *The Servant* (1963) and *Accident* (1967). Bogarde was now in a different league of movie star, being used by Luchino Visconti in *The Damned* (1969) and *Death in Venice*

LEFT *Alec Guinness (1914–2000) was one of the most popular British stars, appearing in a number of Ealing comedies such as* The Man in the White Suit *(1951).*

NOWHERE dare they show themselves

NOWHERE dare they rest . . .

DIRK BOGARDE
HUNTED

with

KAY   ELIZABETH
WALSH · SELLARS

and introducing

JON WHITELEY

Screen play by JACK WHITTINGHAM
Directed by CHARLES CRICHTON
Produced by JULIAN WINTLE
An Independent Artists picture

ABOVE *Dirk Bogarde occasionally won better parts than his usual romantic hero in British movies. In* Hunted *(1952) he played a criminal on the run.*

(1971). He also worked with Alain Resnais in *Providence* (1977) and Bernard Tavernier in *These Foolish Things* (1990). He died in London in 1999.

JULIE ANDREWS (b. 1935)

Andrews made her name in the stage version of *My Fair Lady* but lost out to Audrey Hepburn when the film came along. She has tried hard to cast off

the squeaky-clean image she then gained from *The Sound of Music* and *Mary Poppins*, determinedly trying to create a sexual image for herself in *The Americanization of Emily, Darling Lili, 10, S.O.B., Victor/Victoria* and *The Man Who Loved Women*. However, her essential scrubbed English nanny persona has never really deserted her. She has appeared in several movies directed by her husband, Blake Edwards. She battled cancer in the late 1990s and had a triumphant return to the Broadway stage.

ABOVE *Julie Andrews's biggest success on screen was as the singing governess in* The Sound of Music *(1965).*

RICHARD BURTON (1925–84)

At times Burton was more famous for his off-screen antics than his on-screen performances: his drinking bouts, his marriages to Elizabeth Taylor, and his consumption of luxury goods when he and Taylor were "hot property" in Hollywood. After appearing in a number of forgettable British films, Burton made *My Cousin*

ABOVE *One of Richard Burton's better screen roles was as a British spy in the film version of Len Deighton's* The Spy Who Came in from the Cold *(1965).*

ABOVE *Hollywood occasionally remembered that Richard Burton had once been a highly distinguished stage actor. He played famous American actor Edwin Booth in* Prince of Players *(1955).*

Rachel *in Hollywood, then the first CinemaScope film* The Robe, *followed by* The Desert Rats, Alexander the Great *and* Bitter Victory. *His career took an upturn with* Cleopatra *and his marriage to Taylor – he then became the male half of the Taylor–Burton industry. But decent movies were still few and far between. Possible exceptions, depending on taste, were* Who's Afraid of Virginia Woolf?, The Spy Who Came in from the Cold, The Taming of the Shrew *and* The Comedians. *He played the hero in* Where Eagles Dare *opposite Eastwood, hammed it up as Henry VIII in* Anne of the Thousand Days, *and was awful in awful movies such as* Blackbeard, Exorcist II *and* The Wild Geese. *His last film, 1984, gave him a decent part and he was effective in it. His was a lost talent.*

LAURENCE OLIVIER (1907–89)

Olivier was a great stage and screen actor. One of the few actors to master both mediums, he appeared in British movies such as *Fire over England* and *The Divorce of Lady X* before going to Hollywood to star in *Wuthering Heights* (during the shooting of which Sam Goldwyn complained about this "dirty British actor"). Hollywood, or Greta Garbo, had already rebuffed him by turning him down for a part in *Queen Christina*. He played Max De Winter in *Rebecca* and Darcy in *Pride and Prejudice*, then he starred in and directed *Henry V* and *Hamlet*. Later film triumphs included *Carrie, Richard III* (which he also directed), *Spartacus* and *The Entertainer*. *Sleuth* and *Marathon Man* were the best of the movies he made in the latter part of his movie career, when he tended to take parts for the money, including playing Neil Diamond's father in *The Jazz Singer*. Olivier could have remained a matinée idol, because he had the looks and style for that role, but he wanted to be much more than that.

BELOW *Laurence Olivier as* Hamlet *in the 1948 version of Shakespeare's play, a movie he also directed.*

PETER O'TOOLE (b. 1932)

O'Toole is another of those British actors famous for their drinking and generally self-destructive ways. He became a star after playing *Lawrence of Arabia* in David Lean's film, then played Henry II to Burton's Becket in *Becket*, but also appeared in some stinkers such as *What's New, Pussycat?*, *Casino Royale* and *Goodbye Mr Chips*. *The Lion in Winter* was one of his more

BELOW *Peter O'Toole's big break came when he played Lawrence in* Lawrence of Arabia, *the 1962 epic directed by David Lean.*

SEAN CONNERY (b. 1930)

There is a lot more to Sean Connery than the James Bond tag. Incomparably the best of the Bond actors (although when you consider the competition, that's not saying much), Connery has also worked for Hitchcock in *Marnie*, for Martin Ritt in *The Molly Maguires* and for John Boorman in *Zardoz*. He played an Arab chieftan in *The Wind and the Lion*, where he got away with his Scottish brogue in the desert, and was an elderly Robin Hood in *Robin and Marian*. He returned to the Bond part in 1983 (*Never Say Never Again*), but his career received a great boost with *The Name of the Rose*, *The Untouchables* and *Indiana Jones and the Last Crusade*, in which he played Harrison Ford's father. In the 1990s he remained a top box-office draw, quite an achievement for a man in his 60s whose career had been written off. Movies such as *The Hunt for Red October*, *First Knight*, *The Rock* and *Entrapment* kept him in the first rank. One of the few Scottish actors to make it internationally, Connery has ploughed some of his vast earnings back into helping deprived Scottish youth get a decent start in life.

notable films, but a succession of box-office failures, together with his reputation for boozing, put his film career in jeopardy. On stage he was so bad as *Macbeth* at the Old Vic that people queued to see him go over-the-top every night. His film career was rescued to a certain extent by *The Stunt Man* and *My Favourite Year*. He had something of a success in Bertolucci's *The Last Emperor*, but the movies he made in the 1990s were almost all forgettable. He returned to the London stage with some success in the play about an alcoholic columnist, *Jeffrey Bernard is Unwell*. Omar Sharif called him "the prototype of the ham" and this is an accurate summation, except to say that hamminess sometimes works in particular roles on screen. In 2003 O'Toole was awarded a Lifetime Achievement Oscar.

RICHARD HARRIS (1930–2002)

Harris was a notorious hellraiser, which is usually a euphemistic description used to disguise a harsher reality. After having featured parts in *The Long and the Short and the Tall* (1961) and *Mutiny on the Bounty* (1962), Irish-born Harris achieved star status playing an inarticulate rugby player in Lindsay Anderson's *This Sporting Life* (1963). This gave Harris credibility as a serious actor, and Italian director Antonioni used him in the enigmatic *The Red Desert* (1964). Thereafter,

ABOVE *Richard Harris became a star after his performance in* This Sporting Life *(1963), which was adapted from the novel by David Storey. For many years he lived a life of excess, but he cleaned up his act in the 1980s.*

Harris's career spiralled downwards in terms of the quality of the movies he appeared in, although he was in some commercial successes: *The Heroes of Telemark* (1965), *Camelot* (1967), *A Man Called Horse* (1970) and *Cromwell* (1970). A multitude of mediocre movies followed, the only exceptions being *The Field* (1990), *Unforgiven* (1992) and *Gladiator* (2000). Pauline Kael, the movie critic, wrote of Harris, "He hauls his surly carcass from movie to movie, being dismembered." However, he had a late success as Dumbledore, the wizard headmaster in the first two *Harry Potter* movies.

ABOVE *Albert Finney played Albert Seaton, a working-class rebel, in Karel Reisz's* Saturday Night and Sunday Morning *(1960). The actress is Shirley Ann Field.*

ALBERT FINNEY (b. 1936)

Finney's stage and screen career has been inconsistent because he has decided that there are more things to life than being a successful and famous actor. Hence, his screen appearances have been spasmodic, although some of his performances reveal that he has what it takes to be a really expert movie actor. His first big success was as Albert Seaton, the archetypal working-class rebel figure in *Saturday Night and Sunday Morning*. He was the first of the British stars who could play working-class men with authenticity; hitherto we had to suffer Johnny Mills or Stewart Granger going down-market. Finney had a popular success with *Tom Jones*, but none of his other 1960s

LEFT *Vanessa Redgrave as she appeared in Antonioni's* Blow-Up. *Redgrave has alternated between stage and screen, but has never really established herself as a first-rank movie star.*

movies made much of a mark – including the underrated *Charlie Bubbles* which he directed himself. He was amusing in *Gumshoe*, excruciating as Hercule Poirot in *Murder on the Orient Express*, but compelling in *Shoot the Moon* and *The Dresser*. Too many movies like *Scrooge*, *Annie* and *Under the Volcano* have restricted the number of decent performances he has given on screen. He made *Miller's Crossing* with the Coen brothers, was Julia Roberts' mentor in *Erin Brockovich*, and starred as Winston Churchill in the TV drama *The Gathering Storm*. Finney is a physical actor of great potential; a few times that potential has been tapped.

JULIE CHRISTIE (b. 1941)

Christie came to prominence in the 1963 *Billy Liar* and then won an Oscar for her performance in *Darling*. Her career reached something of a peak with *Doctor Zhivago*, but she was woefully miscast in *Far from the Madding Crowd*. Two better roles came her way in *Petulia* and *The Go-Between*. She co-starred with Warren Beatty in *McCabe and Mrs Miller*, definitely one of her better films, as was Nicolas

ABOVE *In her early days in British movies, Julie Christie had small parts in comedies such as* The Fast Lady. *Here she is with the star of the movie, James Robertson Justice.*

Roeg's *Don't Look Now*. *Shampoo* and *Nashville* were two further hits for her. *Heaven Can Wait*, *Demon Seed*, *Heat and Dust* and Kenneth Branagh's *Hamlet* (in which she played the Queen) were other notable movies.

MICHAEL CAINE (b. 1933)

Caine is a screen actor of extremely limited range who can be effective in some roles. He was best suited to parts such as Harry Palmer in *The Ipcress File* and *Funeral in Berlin*. Other very popular movies he appeared in include *The Italian Job* and *Get Carter*. There was a period in the late 1970s and early 80s when it seemed his career had been sunk by too many bad movies, but *Educating Rita* rescued it. *Hannah and Her Sisters* (for which he won an Oscar), *Dirty Rotten Scoundrels*, *Blood and Wine*, *Little Voice*, *The Cider House Rules* (his second Oscar) and *The Quiet American* have balanced the bad movies he has continued to make. He has survived at the top in the business.

JUDI DENCH (b. 1934)

Dench is by no stretch of the imagination a big movie star, but her infrequent screen appearances have garnered her much praise and not a few awards, including Oscars. Her film career

ABOVE *Michael Caine made a real impact as Harry Palmer, Len Deighton's rebellious British agent, in* The Ipcress File *(1965).*

did not really take off until the 1980s when two adaptations of British novels, *A Room with a View* and *A Handful of Dust* reminded movie-makers she could act on screen. She was 007's handler in the most recent James Bond movies, *GoldenEye*, *Tomorrrow Never Dies*, *The World Is Not*

87

BELOW *Judi Dench as she appeared in 84 Charing Cross Road (1986). She played second lead to Anne Bancroft and Anthony Hopkins in this movie, but went on to carve out a secure niche in the film world as well as continuing her distinguished stage career.*

Enough and *Die Another Day*, played Queen Victoria in *Mrs Brown* and Elizabeth I in *Shakespeare in Love*, for which she was unaccountably given an Oscar. Other movies include *Tea with Mussolini* and *Chocolat*.

ANTHONY HOPKINS (b. 1937)

Hopkins has only intermittently taken his profession totally seriously in the sense of pursuing the great roles and taking care about what he does on screen. He has spoken caustically of the preciousness and pretentiousness of the British theatre and actors, which is refreshing, but too often he has involved himself in crass movie projects; indeed, far too often for a man of his immense talent. His screen career did not really start to take off until he made *Magic* for Richard Attenborough in 1978 and *The Elephant Man* for David Lynch in 1980. He was a convincing Captain Bligh in *The Bounty* (1984), but really made an impression as Hannibal Lecter in *The Silence of the Lambs*. *Howards End*, *The Remains of the Day* and *Shadowlands* were three of his better movies and he also scored playing Nixon in the Oliver Stone movie of that name. Appearing in movies such as *Meet Joe Black*, *The Mask of Zorro* and more appearances as Lecter in *Hannibal* and *Red Dragon* no doubt pays the bills, but these are not worthy of his talents.

EMMA THOMPSON (b. 1959)

Thompson's usual role in movies is that of the eminently sensible but feeling woman, as she showed in *The Remains of the Day*, *Howards End* and *In the Name of the Father*. At one time married to Kenneth Branagh, they seemed for a while to be British filmland's "golden couple", although comparisons with Oliver and Vivien Leigh were surely far-fetched. She played the Bloomsbury Group painter Carrington in the movie of the same name and adapted Jane Austen's *Sense and Sensibility* for the screen in 1995, a movie she also starred in. She was chosen to play the Hillary Clinton-type character in *Primary Colors* (1998).

KENNETH BRANAGH (b. 1960)

Branagh has been involved in a multitude of enterprises, both on stage and on screen. After forging for himself a high-profile career in serious theatre, he directed and starred in *Henry V* (1989), which led to inevitable comparisons with Laurence Olivier and his 1944 movie of Shakespeare's play. He then went to Hollywood and directed a quasi-tribute to *film noir*, *Dead Again*, before acting in and directing the indulgent *Peter's Friends*. A second Shakespeare movie, *Much Ado About Nothing*, was another success, which was followed by a full-length *Hamlet*, packed full of Hollywood and British stars. His acting career rocketed with critically acclaimed performances in two television dramas, *Conspiracy* (2001) and *Shackleton* (2002), followed by a movie role in *Harry Potter and the Chamber of Secrets* (2002).

LEFT *Anthony Hopkins will be remembered as Hannibal Lecter in* The Silence of the Lambs, Hannibal *and* Red Dragon.

ABOVE *Emma Thompson starred alongside Hugh Grant and Kate Winslet in* Sense and Sensibility. *Her script won her an Oscar.*

PIERCE BROSNAN (b. 1951)

Brosnan had made *The Fourth Protocol* and *Mrs Doubtfire* before being chosen as James Bond in succession to Timothy Dalton and appearing in *GoldenEye* (1995). He has followed that up with more Bond movies, *Tomorrow Never Dies* (1997), *The World Is Not Enough* (1999) and *Die Another Day* (2002). An Irishman, he usually plays suave on screen, but has sent up that image in *Doubtfire* and *Mars Attacks!* The 2003 *Evelyn* was an attempt to break away from the Bond image: he played a father fighting for custody of his daughter.

HELENA BONHAM CARTER (b. 1966)

At the start of her screen career, Bonham Carter was closely associated with Merchant-Ivory productions, such as *A Room with a View*, *Where Angels Fear to Tread* and *Howards End*. She usually plays a slightly neurotic variation of the English rose and can be irritatingly affected doing it. She was in the Branagh-directed *Mary Shelley's Frankenstein*, Woody Allen's *Mighty Aphrodite* and a film version of Henry James's *Wings of a Dove*. Generally associated with period movies, she has tried to break free from that image in *Fight Club*, *Women Talking Dirty* and *Planet of the Apes*.

ABOVE *Helena Bonham Carter with co-star Rupert Graves in a scene from* Where Angels Fear to Tread *(1991), a film adaptation of E.M. Forster's first novel.*

RALPH FIENNES (b. 1962)

Fiennes is one of the outstanding British stage actors to have emerged since around 1990, and he has carried that success over into his screen roles. He first made an impact as Heathcliff in the 1992 *Wuthering Heights*, but made his major screen breakthrough in Spielberg's *Schindler's List* playing a sadistic Nazi. He was then directed by Robert Redford in *Quiz Show* as an Ivy League intellectual caught up in the grubby corruption of 1950s American

ABOVE *Ralph Fiennes' performance as a Nazi officer in* Schindler's List *won him a well-deserved Oscar nomination.*

game shows, and won international acclaim as the burned plane-crash victim in *The English Patient*. The one blot on his screen record is playing John Steed in *The Avengers*, but *Onegin* and *The End of the Affair* put him back on track. He was excellent in *Sunshine*, a European co-production directed by Istvan Szabo in which he played three parts, each a member of a different generation of a Hungarian Jewish family. He is a fine, intelligent actor at home on stage or screen, but needs to avoid movies like *Maid in Manhattan*.

KATE WINSLET (b. 1975)

Winslet's big break came with *Sense and Sensibility* (1995), but she really hit the big time starring with Leonardo DiCaprio in *Titanic*. Movies such as *Hideous Kinky, Holy Smoke, Quills* and *The Life of David Gale* did not do much for her career, but she received critical acclaim in 2004 for *Eternal Sunshine of the Spotless Mind* and *Finding Neverland*.

JUDE LAW (b. 1972)

Law played Lord Alfred Douglas opposite Stephen Fry's Oscar Wilde in the 1997 *Wilde*, then had successes in *Gattaca* and *eXistenZ*. He was very good as a nasty, spoiled rich kid in *The Talented Mr Ripley*, and had another unsympathetic role in *Road to Perdition*. His talent has established him as a star, with roles in *Cold Mountain, Alfie, Closer* and *The Aviator* doing him no harm.

EWAN MCGREGOR (b. 1971)

McGregor had major successes in two movies directed by compatriot Danny Boyle: *Shallow Grave* (1994) and *Trainspotting* (1996). He managed to survive being miscast in *Emma* (and wearing a terrible wig) and followed that with *Brassed Off, A Life Less Ordinary, Velvet Goldmine, Little Voice* and *Rogue Trader*. He then took the Hollywood shilling by appearing as the young Obi-Wan Kenobi in the first episodes of the *Star Wars* series. He also appeared in *Black Hawk Down* directed by Ridley Scott. McGregor shows no inhibitions on screen at all and he dared to sing in *Moulin Rouge* (2001), emerging with credit.

CATHERINE ZETA-JONES (b. 1969)

Zeta-Jones emerged from the musical stage and appeared in *Christopher Columbus: The Discovery, Splitting Heirs, Blue Juice* and *The Phantom*. She followed that with *The Mark of Zorro, Entrapment, Traffic* (the one worthwhile movie she has starred in) and *America's Sweethearts*. She made a well-publicized marriage to American star Michael Douglas in 2000 and won a Best Supporting Actress Oscar for her singing role in *Chicago* (2002).

89

ABOVE *Welsh-born Catherine Zeta-Jones as she appeared in the 1996 Paramount movie* The Phantom.

FRENCH STARS

JEAN GABIN (1904–76)

Jean Gabin could play proletarian heroes, tough guys and members of the officer class. He starred in some of the great French classics: *La Grande Illusion*, *Le Quai des Brumes*, *La Bête Humaine* and *Le Jour Se Lève*. He frequently played gangsters in movies such as *Touchez pas au Grisbi* and *The Sicilian*. He also played Inspector Maigret in a series of movies, but there is no doubt that it will be for the pre-war movies that Gabin will be best remembered. In these films he seemed to typify something essentially French: style and toughness mixed with tenderness, honesty and a romantic aura.

YVES MONTAND (1921–91)

Gabin's natural successor, Montand started as a singer, then graduated to serious roles. He first came to international prominence in *The Wages of Fear* (1953). He made *Let's Make Love* (1960) with Marilyn Monroe and had a much-publicized affair with her. However, his Hollywood career did

BELOW *Yves Montand took over the mantle of Jean Gabin and became for many the screen's archetypal Frenchman. In actual fact Montand was born Ivo Levi and was Italian by birth. When he died, France went into mourning.*

not take off and he returned to Europe to make films such as *The War is Over*, *Vivre pour Vivre*, *The Red Circle* and *Le Sauvage*. He returned to Hollywood in 1970 to make *On a Clear Day You Can See Forever* with Streisand and Vincente Minnelli. In the latter part of his career he had great success with *Jean de Florette* and *Manon des Sources*. Montand died in 1991 at the age of 70. The French mourned him deeply; most people remembered him as the young protégé of Edith Piaf, the errant but loving husband of Simone Signoret and as a French Bogart.

SIMONE SIGNORET (1921–85)

One of those French actresses who seemed to symbolize something eternally French, Signoret had a long and distinguished career in French movies from 1942 to 1982. Her best-known films are *La Ronde*, *Casque d'Or*, *Les Diaboliques* and *La Mort en ce Jardin*. Foreign films included *Room at the Top*, *Ship of Fools*, *The Deadly Affair* and *Games*.

ABOVE *Brigitte Bardot first came to prominence in Roger Vadim's* And God Created Woman. *Here she is seen with co-star Curt Jurgens.*

BRIGITTE BARDOT (b. 1934)

Bardot became a sex symbol in the 1950s, largely due to her roles in movies directed by her then-husband, Roger Vadim: *And God Created Woman* and *Heaven Fell That Night*. Dubbed a "sex kitten", Bardot never managed to break free from that stereotype, although she tried in movies such as *The Truth*, *Contempt* and *Shalako*. In her latter years she practically disowned her movie career, preferring to battle for the rights of animals and being connected with extreme right-wing politics in France.

PHILIPPE NOIRET (b. 1930)

Noiret has become better known internationally through performances in recently successful films, *Life and Nothing But* and *Cinema Paradiso*, but he has had a screen career spanning four decades. He was in *La Grande Bouffe* (*Blow Out*), Francesco Rosi's *Three Brothers* and Tavernier's *The Clockmaker*. He has appeared in Hitchcock's *Topaz*, *Justine*, *Murphy's War* and *Round Midnight*. He had a success in *Il Postino* in 1994. He has become almost as recognizable a symbol of Frenchness as Gabin was in his day.

ABOVE *Philippe Noiret's most famous movie is probably* Cinema Paradiso. *Here he is on the set of the movie (far left) with co-stars Salvatore Cascio and Jacques Perrin.*

JEANNE MOREAU (b. 1928)

Moreau came to prominence with *Les Amants* (1958) and *Les Liaisons Dangereuses* (1959). Antonioni used her beautiful but ravaged features in *La Notte* and Truffaut saw her as a symbol of femininity in *Jules et Jim*. She worked with Luis Buñuel in *Diary of a Chambermaid* and Orson Welles in *Chimes at Midnight*. She has continued to work in movies well into her 70s.

GÉRARD DEPARDIEU (b. 1948)

Depardieu has graduated from animalistic parts to portraying more sensitive men in *Le Dernier Métro*, *The Woman Next Door*, *Danton*, *Jean de Florette*, *Trop Belle pour Toi*, *Cyrano de Bergerac*, *Green Card* and *Uranus*. Indeed, the hulk has turned out to be a fine screen actor. He was unable to

ABOVE *Gérard Depardieu had a huge success starring in* Jean de Florette *(1986), directed by Claude Berri.*

avoid *1492* being the turkey it was, however, but *Tous les Matins du Monde*, *Germinal*, *Colonel Chabert* and *The Horseman on the Roof* were better for him and he has remained at the top.

CATHERINE DENEUVE (b. 1943)

Deneuve became a symbol of French beauty in art-house movies such as *Les Parapluies de Cherbourg*, *Les Demoiselles de Rochefort*, *Mayerling* and *The Hunger*. Polanski used her rather differently in *Repulsion*. Luis Buñuel also gave her more opportunity than usual in *Belle de Jour* and then in *Tristana*, while François Truffaut starred her in *Le Sauvage* and *Le Dernier Métro*. She has performed in several American movies including *Mayerling* and *The April Fools*, but she has never seriously threatened to become a Hollywood star. She had a success with *Indochine* and was not reluctant to play her age and an alcoholic in *Place Vendôme* (1998).

ISABELLE HUPPERT (b. 1955)

Huppert emerged as one of the leading screen actresses in France in the 1970s and 80s. Her first big success was as the victim heroine of *The Lacemaker*, then she had a change of pace as the murderer, *Violette Nozière*. Cimino followed this change of style by casting her as the gun-toting madame in *Heaven's Gate*. Her lack of classical beauty and her limited English may mean that international stardom will elude her, but she still commands strong parts, as she showed playing the title role in Claude Chabrol's version of Flaubert's classic novel, *Madame Bovary*. She was kept busy in French movies in the 1990s and should still be cast in leading roles because she is an accomplished actress.

JULIETTE BINOCHE (b. 1964)

Binoche first came to international attention when she appeared in *The Unbearable Lightness of Being* (1988), which she followed with *Les Amants du Pont-Neuf*. Louis Malle directed her as the havoc-causing heroine of *Damage*.

ABOVE *Juliette Binoche starred in Krzysztof Kieslowski's* Three Colours *trilogy –* Blue *(1993),* White *(1994) and* Red *(1994).*

91

She won an Academy Award for *The English Patient* (1996) and had a great success with *Chocolat* (2000). She was also very effective in the fine period drama *Widow of Saint-Pierre* (2000). Because of her looks, she is sometimes not taken very seriously by critics, but the fact is that she is an intelligent and effective actress when the role is right.

DANIEL AUTEUIL (b. 1950)

It was with *Jean de Florette* and *Manon des Sources* that Auteuil made his name, but since then he has played convincingly in *Un Coeur en Hiver*, *My Favourite Season* and *La Reine Margot*. Auteuil can communicate power and vulnerability on screen and is certainly one of the very best screen actors around.

ITALIAN STARS

ANNA MAGNANI (1907–73)

Magnani played powerful, passionate women to the hilt. There was never underplaying when she was on screen, but she was highly effective in Rossellini's *Open City* and De Sica's *The Miracle*. In her Italian movies she seemed to encapsulate the incendiary, sensual stereotype of Italian womanhood, but in fact she was an able actress. Hollywood tried to make an international star of her in movies such as *The Rose Tattoo*, *Wild is the Wind* and *The Fugitive Kind* (with Marlon Brando), but she could never really be fitted into the Hollywood mould. After her Hollywood efforts, she failed to regain her former status in her domestic industry and died at the comparatively early age of 66. She was seemingly as incendiary off-screen as she was on-screen.

GINA LOLLOBRIGIDA (b. 1927)

"La Lollo", as she was known, was, unlike Magnani, never accused of overacting; indeed, the debate was whether she ever acted at all. She played mindless, busty and plastic beauties in a succession of movies of which *Fanfan la Tulipe*, *Les Belles de Nuit*, *Bread, Love and Dreams*, *Beat the Devil*, *Trapeze*, *Solomon and Sheba* and *Woman*

of *Straw* were the most successful. As she advanced in years, her career fizzled out, having had no track record as an actress to sustain it. Her screen image must have set back the cause of the liberation of Italian women for many years.

LEFT *Anna Magnani was one of the most powerful actresses of the Italian cinema, but Hollywood didn't utilize her talents properly.*

BELOW *Gina Lollobrigida was one of the most popular Italian stars of the 1950s and 60s. At her peak, she was the Italian glamour star.*

ABOVE *Here Gina Lollobrigida is seen with French co-star Daniel Gelin in the 1954 production* Woman of Rome.

MARCELLO MASTROIANNI (1923–96)

A romantic star who was also an intelligent actor, Mastroianni worked memorably with Fellini in *La Dolce Vita* and *8½* and Antonioni in *La Notte*. Other important films included *The Stranger*, *Yesterday, Today and Tomorrow*, *Casanova '70*, *La Grande Bouffe* and, with Fellini again, *Fred and Ginger*. There is no doubt that Mastroianni occasionally took roles he could amble through, but he generally brought a skilful technique to his screen appearances. Perhaps his good looks meant that he would inevitably be cast in rather silly romantic stories, but at his best he could be very effective when working with able directors who recognized what he was capable of.

SOPHIA LOREN (b. 1934)

"La Loren" has her supporters who say she is a talented actress. These fans cite movies such as *Desire Under the Elms*, *Two Women* and *The Condemned of Altona* as evidence of this. But the public mostly remember her for her exposure in movies such as *Boy on a*

ABOVE *Marcello Mastroianni was at his most effective on screen when he made movies with directors such as Antonioni. Here he starred in* La Notte *(1961) opposite Jeanne Moreau. The movie is a bleak picture of a loveless marriage.*

ABOVE *Carlo Ponti married Sophia Loren twice (1957 and 1966) and he produced many of her movies, including* Ghosts Italian Style *(1968).*

ABOVE *Sophia Loren had a great success appearing opposite Peter Sellers in a film version of Bernard Shaw's play,* The Millionairess *(1960).*

Dolphin, *Heller in Pink Tights*, *El Cid*, *The Millionairess*, *Arabesque* and *Man of La Mancha*. Married to producer Carlo Ponti, Loren has had her difficulties with the Italian tax authorities, spending a short spell in jail. She has a cold quality on screen which prevents her, for some, from being watchable. However, she was an international star for a number of years. Even in her 70s, La Loren still flaunts it and is always more than capable of arousing fan frenzy among those who worship her.

93

LINO VENTURA (1919–87)

Italian-born Lino Ventura made as many French movies as Italian, starring in some of Jean-Pierre Melville's most memorable gangster flicks: *Second Wind* (*Le Deuxième Souffle*), *Le Samouraï* and *The Red Circle*. His deadpan style was very well suited to the ultra-cool anti-heroes of Melville's fables of the criminal world. Claude Lelouch also used Ventura in *La Bonne Année*, which cast Ventura in a more romantic role. Ventura was in the Bogart mould and the enduring image one has of him is in a trench coat in shadowy rooms or walking down dark streets.

INDEX

ACKNOWLEDGEMENTS

The publisher would like to thank the following for the use of their pictures:

Cine Art Gallery
759 Fulham Road
London SW6 5UU

Vertigo Gallery
29 Bedfordbury
Covent Garden
London WC2N 4BJ

Moviedrome
moviedrome@ntlworld.com